THE SOCIAL POLICY OF
NAZI GERMANY

THE SOCIAL POLICY
OF
NAZI GERMANY

BY

C. W. GUILLEBAUD

NEW YORK

Howard Fertig

1971

First published in 1941

HOWARD FERTIG, INC. EDITION 1971
Published by arrangement with the Cambridge University Press

Library of Congress Catalog Card Number: 71-80553

PRINTED IN THE UNITED STATES OF AMERICA
BY NOBLE OFFSET PRINTERS, INC.

"The outlook as regards [German] public opinion in April, 1939, from the Nazi point of view was rather good. Reports from the big and fairly representative cities shewed a general contentment among the working classes."

Searchlight on Europe (p. 126),

John de Courcy.

*   *   *   *

"Those who make a total claim to the soul of a people must not content themselves with advocating their principles, but must also possess a gift for organisation."

Dr Ley, in *Germany Speaks* (p. 184).

*   *   *   *

"For what shall it profit a man, if he shall gain the whole world, and lose his own soul?"   St Mark viii. 36.

*   *   *   *

The democratic ideal is "a doctrine that the interest of the commonwealth is greater than that of any part or class, and yet that no part may be neglected in the computation of the whole; that no man is too great to be subject to the law, and none too small to enjoy its protection; that all opinions are entitled to a hearing, but none may be imposed on the unwilling; that authority is the only safeguard of freedom, and the liberties of the subject the only abiding foundation on which authority can rest."   *The Times*, 2 November, 1940.

PREFACE

WHEN I was asked by the Editor of this series to write this little book, I realised that it would be a very difficult task to accomplish satisfactorily under war conditions; partly because access to material is restricted to what is available in this country, and partly because the war makes it doubly hard to maintain that objectivity which alone would make such a book either worth writing or reading. I cannot hope always to have succeeded, but where I have failed, it has not been for lack of endeavour.

The subject-matter of the book, for the most part, covers the period from 1933 to September 1939. The material has been drawn chiefly from official German sources and from the publications of the International Labour Office, but I have also taken into account any material of an adverse or critical nature which has come to my notice.

I desire to express my sincere thanks to Dr Ernest Barker and Mr E. A. G. Robinson for reading my proofs and for making a number of helpful suggestions.

C. W. GUILLEBAUD

St John's College
　　Cambridge
October 1940

CONTENTS

CHAPTER V

CHAPTER VI

CHAPTER VII

CHAPTER VIII

THE SOCIAL POLICY OF
NAZI GERMANY

CHAPTER I

THE HISTORICAL BACKGROUND

THE social policy[1] of National Socialist Germany is in part a continuance of past traditions and measures inherited from the Germany which it replaced, and in part consists of innovations which reflect the new ideas and the spirit of National Socialism.

IMPERIAL GERMANY

Social legislation on a comprehensive scale in Germany may be said to date from the Industrial Code, passed in 1869 and applied to all parts of

[1] Social policy may be defined as intervention by the State or other public authority for the purpose of improving the conditions of life and work of the people. This is deliberately a narrow definition, as in the wider sense in which it is often used by German writers it can be made to embrace virtually the whole field of economic policy, every institution and activity in the economic sphere being assessed in its relation to the State, which in turn is regarded as the integration of the life of the people in all its aspects. Those National Socialists who lay so much stress on this wider interpretation of social policy are following a peculiarly German tradition in this respect, and one which differs widely from that prevailing in our own country.

the North German Confederation, and after 1871, to the whole German Reich. This Code in turn embodied many of the regulations of the Prussian Code of 1839, but its chief weakness consisted in the absence of proper provisions for inspection and enforcement. This weakness was not rectified until 1891, when a new and much more comprehensive Industrial Code was drawn up, though it is noteworthy that inspection was still not centralised, but was left to the individual States. By 1914 successive amendments had brought the legal protection of Labour to a high level of effectiveness, comparable with that in any other Western country.

It was, however, in the field of social insurance and not of factory legislation that Germany showed herself a pioneer. As early as 1881, Bismarck, anxious to find a constructive reply to the socialism which was making such headway amongst the German workers, and desirous also of checking the tide of emigration (221,000 in the single year 1881), introduced a compulsory Accident Insurance Bill. The Bill met with opposition and had to be withdrawn. In 1883 a compulsory Sickness Insurance Act was passed, and this was followed by an amended Accident Insurance Act in 1884 and by an Old Age and Invalidity Insurance Act in 1889.

Bismarck himself must probably be regarded from this point of view more as a political opportunist than as a genuine social reformer. The main inspiration for the new trend of German social policy, which began in the 'eighties of the nineteenth century, was the *Verein für Sozialpolitik* founded in 1872 by the "Socialists of the Chair" (*Kathedersozialisten*), e.g. Schmoller, Wagner, Knapp and Brentano, with whom were later associated Max Weber and Bücher. It was these men who drove home the idea of the State as a social trustee, and who sought to change even the name of Political Economy to that of Social Economy. Their ideas were shared and to some extent carried into practical effect by a small group of outstanding civil servants, e.g. Bötticher, Lohmann, Berlepsch and Count Posadowsky.

Long in advance of any other country, therefore, the German worker found himself at least partially protected against the risks of sickness, accident and invalidity, and provided with a modest pension in his old age. The Marxist challenge that "the worker has no country" was met by staking out a claim for him in his own country; and small though it was, there can be no doubt that it went some way towards meeting an urgent social and political need. The whole system was codified and extended by the Insurance Code of 1911, at which date the annual cost was £57,500,000, of which, however, only £4,000,000 came from public funds, the remainder being borne by contributions from employers and employees.

Unemployment under the Empire was dealt with partly by municipal labour exchanges, which were set up in almost all important industrial centres, partly by special lodging houses (*Herbergen*) and public relief stations (*Verpflegungsstationen*) reserved only for the unemployed, and partly by municipal subsidies to trade union unemployment insurance funds (the so-called Ghent scheme).

It must be remembered that Germany was in a phase of rapid industrial expansion before 1914 and that most unemployment was only of short duration, due chiefly to seasonal and frictional causes; hence the measures just referred to were less inadequate than might at first sight appear. In spite of Germany's priority in the field of social insurance, she was slow in applying a general measure of insurance for unemployment. As late as 1912, the year after the passing of the British National Insurance Act (Part II of which established a partial experimental scheme for compulsory insurance against unemployment), the German Imperial Government in a formal statement declared that no basis had yet been discovered for Imperial insurance against unemployment which could be considered acceptable.

Apart from the specific provisions for relieving unemployment there remained the poor law, which was organised in unions on lines not unlike those prevailing in Britain, although the administration was less negative and outdoor relief was more freely given. The Elberfeld system of the supervision of relief by voluntary unpaid workers was adopted in almost all towns throughout Germany, and this, combined with the beneficial effects of social insurance and of a relatively enlightened housing policy, resulted in a conspicuous absence of the more extreme forms of destitution which characterised other industrial countries.

Private charity existed on a considerable scale in Germany, but was not nearly so widespread as in Great Britain, municipal and public services for the relief of poverty being far more general in the former than in the latter country.

Trade unions were slow to develop in Germany. The Industrial Code of 1869 had legalised combinations in Germany, and they possessed the right to strike, but Bismarck's anti-socialist law of 1878 nearly wrecked the movement. With the repeal of the law in 1890 trade unions went ahead fast, and although their freedom of action was still much restricted by legislative and administrative measures, they had a membership of three millions by 1913. The unions were strongly influenced by political considerations and were regarded by most of the employers with open hostility and by the State with a thinly veiled suspicion. It was not until as late as 1906–14 that collective bargaining began to play any considerable role in industrial relations, and at the latter date the unions were still struggling—often vainly—for recognition by the employers.

Finally, mention must be made of the educational system. The basis of this was elementary education which, in Prussia and Saxony at least, had been compulsory since the Napoleonic wars, and which was supplemented for the ordinary worker by a highly developed system of continuation schools. For the foremen and some of the higher grades of artisan there were the trade schools, and for the technical experts the secondary schools, State technical high schools and Universities. Coupled with compulsory military service the result was an educational system which was not merely one of the greatest factors in Germany's industrial leadership in many branches of industry, but also constituted a social force of the utmost importance.

To sum up: the attitude of the State in Imperial

Germany was a mixture of paternalism and humanitarianism. While on the one hand it did not interfere in the conflict between labour and capital for a share in the product of industry, on the other hand it protected labour in the factory and the workshop, and above all it sought to give to the worker a measure of security against some of the economic and social risks incidental to modern industrialism. Social insurance thus sub-served the same aim as the educational system—that of producing good citizens and promoting national strength and efficiency.

THE WEIMAR REPUBLIC

The Weimar Constitution of August 1919 brought fundamental changes in that sphere of social policy from which the State had deliberately kept aloof in Imperial Germany—the sphere of industrial relations. The World War had already given a big stimulus to collective bargaining and had greatly strengthened the power of the trade unions, but the new Constitution gave organised labour a legal status such as existed in no other country.

Article 157 put labour under the special protection of the Reich. Article 159 guaranteed the right of combination for the protection and promotion of labour and economic conditions to everybody and to all professions. Article 163 declared that "every German has...the moral duty so to use his intellectual and physical powers as is demanded by the welfare of the community. Every German shall have the opportunity to earn his living by productive labour. So long as suitable employment cannot be found for him, his maintenance shall be provided for." Finally, legal recognition was given to the collective agreement in Article 165: "Wage earners and salaried employees are authorised to co-operate on equal terms with the employers in the regulation of wages and working conditions, as well as in the entire economic development of the productive forces. The organisations on both sides and the agreements between them are recognised."

To carry out the provisions of these Articles of the Constitution, an enormous mass of detailed legislation, covering almost every aspect of labour relations, was passed by the Republic.

Most important, both in theory and practice, was the new status of the collective contract. Agreements freely entered into by the employers' and workers' organisations were binding on both parties and were legally enforceable. Moreover, power was given by the Ministry of Labour to extend the terms of an existing agreement to a whole industry if such "contracts acquired a dominant importance in the shaping of working conditions in that area". The result was a great expansion of collective bargaining throughout German industry. While the number of employees working under collective contracts before the World War fluctuated around two millions, in the years of the Weimar Republic the number was between twelve and fourteen millions.

Disputes of an individual character arising out of the labour contract were referred as a rule to special Labour Courts (*Arbeitsgerichte*) whose decision was final; while collective disputes were referred to Mediation Boards (*Schlichtungsausschüsse*). If the award of a Mediation Board was accepted by both parties, it became a collective agreement and, as such, had legal effect. If the award was rejected by either side, it might still be declared binding by a State Mediator (*Schlichter*) or by the Ministry of Labour. In the later years of the Republic, an increasing use was made of these reserved powers, and in some industries, e.g. the metal, textile and mining industries, the wages and working conditions of between two-thirds and three-quarters of the total numbers employed came to be regulated by compulsory awards. As the trade unions were powerful during most of this period, and the mediation authorities were in general sympathetic to the claims of labour, while industrial conditions were improving on the whole from 1925 onwards, the net result was a steadily rising level of wages, which reinforced the inflationary tendencies of the time.[1] Indeed, wages continued to rise even after the boom had broken in 1929, and it was not until the Emergency Decrees of December 1931, under Brüning, that there was any appreciable break in the general wage level.

Inside the factory or other business unit, Works Councils composed of elected representatives of the workers only were established, which were entrusted with extensive legal powers. The Works Council was required to co-operate (in an advisory capacity) with the employers in promoting efficiency of production, in maintaining peace within the establishment, in agreeing on works rules with the employees, etc. It also had the important power of investigating dismissals and could, if it considered that the employers had acted without "due cause", take such cases to the Labour Court for final decision. If the Court ruled that the dismissal was unjustifiable, it could compel the employer to choose between the alternatives of re-employing the man or compensating him on a scale fixed by the Court. The underlying conception of co-operation between employers and workers was further extended by the right given

[1] J. W. Angell, *The Recovery of Germany*, 2nd ed. pp. 283-4.

to the Works Council to elect one or two representatives to sit on the supervisory boards
(*Aufsichtsräte*) of all companies, and also, in the
case of the bigger concerns, to receive a balance
sheet and profit-and-loss account of the establishment for the previous year. On paper the Works
Councils were one of the most interesting and important of the innovations of the Weimar Republic
in the sphere of industrial relations; for here appeared to be a genuine and novel attempt to further
the ideal of industrial democracy. But it must be
admitted that the reality fell a long way below
the ideal. The provisions for representation on
the supervisory boards of companies were never
much more than a mere formality. In the larger
undertakings the Works Councils proved themselves a useful if subordinate piece of industrial
machinery, though they never had much real
power and became almost wholly impotent during
the depression of 1930–32. In the smaller works employing less than fifty men it became increasingly
common, even in the boom period of 1927–29,
when the first novelty had worn off, for them not
to be elected at all. If the Republic had lasted
longer the Works Councils might have developed
in time into an important institution; they certainly
were not entitled to be so described when the
National Socialists swept them away in 1933.

Already before 1914, German factory legislation had been brought to a high level and, with one exception, the changes since 1918 were of minor importance. The exception consisted in the introduction of a general eight-hour working day, which was first promulgated in a decree of November 1918. Detailed legislation followed in 1919, but an amending Act of 1923 provided for so many exceptions that little more than the principle was left of the eight-hour day. A later Act of 1927, however, restored the eight-hour day as a normal maximum over the greater part of German industry, though still with many loopholes for the working of longer hours.

To the Weimar Republic belongs the credit for the extension of the social insurance system to unemployment in 1927 and for a number of interesting innovations in connection with the relief and prevention of unemployment.

Prior to 1927 relief was granted to the unemployed at first by the Reich, the States and the local authorities, and from October 1923 by contributions from workers and employers supplemented by subsidies from public funds. Some light on the extent of inflation in Germany is thrown by the fact that the *daily* rate of unemployment relief on 19 November 1923 ranged, according to the locality, from 630 to 780,000,000,000 marks, which were the equivalent of less than one shilling. In 1927 the Employment Exchanges and Unemployment Insurance Act was passed. As in Great Britain, the system was based on the Employment Exchanges, the scope of which had already been widened in 1922 and which now became a co-ordinated Federal Service. The Act provided for equal compulsory contributions from employers and workers, both contributions and benefits being made to vary with wages. While no regular contribution was made from public funds to ordinary insurance benefit (apart from provisions for loans to cover possible deficits), emergency unemployment allowances to those who had exhausted their normal benefit were supported from public funds. The finance of the un-employment insurance fund had been based on an assumed average figure of 1,200,000 unemployed. But the Act had only been in force for two years when the collapse of the boom of 1927–29 brought with it unemployment on such a scale as had never before been experienced. It was found necessary to raise contributions and drastically to cut down benefits; while by July 1932 the maximum dura-tion of ordinary benefit (originally twenty-six weeks) had been reduced to six weeks, after which a means test was imposed. As the number of unemployed increased, the proportion cared for by ordinary benefit diminished. In the last nine months of 1932 only 15 % of the unemployed received ordinary benefit in spite of very large Government loans (in effect subsidies), 25 % received emergency allowances, 40 % were on poor relief, while 20 % received neither benefit nor relief. During this period unemployment was over five millions. The unemployment insurance system in Germany therefore broke down even more completely than in Great Britain.

Already in the pre-insurance period, 1919 to 1926, considerable use had been made both of public works and of relief works as a means of providing employment for those who would otherwise have been unemployed. The finance for these works was found partly from Federal and State sources and partly from the unemployment assistance funds, i.e. from the joint contributions of employers and workers for the relief of unemployment. Under the Insurance Act of 1927 this "productive unemployment relief" was systematised and incorporated as an integral part of the system. The Statutory Labour Board (*Reichsanstalt für Arbeitsvermittlung und Arbeitslosenversicherung*) was empowered to make subsidies to public bodies to enable them to undertake works employing persons eligible for unemployment benefits. The normal practice at this time was to

pay the current local rate of wages to those employed on such works, and it was found that the
direct cost of providing work in this manner was
often as much as four times that of their maintenance as unemployed. Against this, however,
must be set the secondary employment arising
from the extra consumption of materials, etc. As
the finances of the National Exchequer and of the
Labour Board were very badly hit by the depression,
the extent to which funds could be used for relief
and public works was necessarily limited, and the
average annual expenditure on arranging relief
work by the Labour Board for the three years
1930–32 was only 30,000,000 marks (£1,500,000).
The principle, however, of using unemployment
insurance funds for the creation of employment
was novel and important, and due credit for it
must be given to the Weimar Republic.

Very late in the reign of the Republic—too late
to rescue it from destruction—much more am-
bitious schemes of employment creation were
devised under von Papen and von Schleicher in
the autumn of 1932. In the first place, provision
was made for the issue on a large scale of tax-
remission certificates (232 million marks of these
certificates were in circulation in December 1932);
secondly, programmes were drawn up for the
expenditure of over 1200 million marks on the

railways, post-office and other public works, which were to be financed predominantly by a new type of employment creation bills discountable by the banks and the Reichsbank. The latter of these two measures became later the basis of the upswing of German industry and trade under the Nazi Government.[1]

Finally, still in the field of employment policy, there remains to mention the system of Labour Service and labour camps. Initially these camps for unemployed were entirely managed by voluntary organisations. Beginning on a very small scale, run mainly by student bodies, they rapidly developed into a nation-wide movement. They were recognised officially by a Decree of July 1931 and were placed under the control of the *Reichsanstalt*, which maintained them out of its funds. In November 1932 as many as 285,000 men were working in the labour camps.

The end of the war in 1918 found Germany suffering from an acute housing shortage and great efforts were made in the succeeding years to remedy this deficiency. Between 1919 and the end of 1932 the *net* increase in dwellings amounted to 2,650,000, and in the year 1929 alone the increase was 317,682, a higher figure, except for the year 1937 (320,057), than any attained under the Nazi régime. About

[1] Cf. C. W. Guillebaud, *The Economic Recovery of Germany*, 1933 *to* 1938.

half the total capital sums needed to finance this building scheme was provided by the State either in the form of loans and subsidies or from the proceeds of a tax on the rent of dwellings already in existence. The housing shortage was most acute in the large cities, and it was there that the chief effort was concentrated. Though much was done to encourage the building of small houses, especially in the outskirts of the cities, a rather high proportion of the total consisted of large blocks of tenement buildings. At the same time, land settlement, particularly in the agricultural east, was pushed on with some vigour, and *Randsiedlung*, or marginal settlement (the transfer of workers, particularly the unemployed, from the centre of cities to the agricultural outskirts), was fostered by the State.

The Weimar Republic, like the Nazi régime which succeeded it, though with a very different spirit, asserted the claim of the State to a decisive voice in the education of its citizens. Article 148 of the Constitution states: "In every school the educational aims must be moral training, public spirit, personal and vocational fitness, and, above all, the cultivation of German national character and of the spirit of national reconciliation." Private preparatory schools were abolished and attendance at public elementary schools was made compulsory for all children. Compulsory education was also provided at continuation schools (of a technical or commercial character) up to the completion of the eighteenth year, and grants were made from public funds to children considered suitable for training in secondary and higher schools, till their education was completed. Adult education in the new *Volkshochschulen*, or People's Universities, was also provided on an extensive scale.

Looking back on the Germany of the Weimar Republic, we see a State, sorely tried both from within and without, lacking above all in internal unity of purpose, and finally brought to ruin by the greatest economic depression of modern times. In its short existence it had endeavoured, not without a considerable measure of success, to justify the title of "The Social Service State". With its many mistakes which contributed to its downfall we are not here concerned, but the foregoing summary shows that it had solid achievements to its credit in the field of social policy, and much that it initiated bore fruit later under the Nazi régime. Moreover, it must not be forgotten that during seven out of its fourteen years of rule— the liquidation of the war from the end of 1918 to 1921, inflation from 1921 to the latter part of 1923, and extreme depression from 1930 to the end of 1932—the normal administration of the State was virtually paralysed.

CHAPTER II

LABOUR POLICY AND INDUSTRIAL
RELATIONS

On 30 January 1933 Hitler assumed office as Chancellor of the German Reich. One of the earliest actions of the new régime in the sphere of labour policy was to abolish all the existing trade unions and to take over their investments and other assets. The ideological motive behind this measure lay in the fact that by far the greater proportion of the trade unions paid at least lip service to Marxian socialism. However little the mass of German labour may have understood the works of Karl Marx, it was as a whole (excluding the Catholics) imbued with the doctrine of the class struggle, which was anathema to the National Socialists. Inheriting as they did a country which was rent with internal strife, their fundamental aim was to impose and enforce a unity as quickly as possible. In place of a labour solidarity which, though incomplete, was nevertheless a living force in the Weimar Republic, they envisaged a national solidarity in which the class struggle was to have no place. After an initial period of some hesitation

during which a section of the leaders of the party
toyed with the idea of establishing a fully cor-
porative State, it was decided to maintain the broad
lines of the existing industrial structure, subject to
a large measure of State control. But it should be
noted that abolition of the trade unions had been
accompanied by the dissolution of all employers'
organisations which had been established for
collective bargaining and for contesting the claims
of labour. By October 1934 the whole vast system
of trade unions had been completely reorganised
and unified in an entirely different form, the
Labour Front, about which more will be said
later.

THE NATIONAL LABOUR LAW

The new status of labour in the State was laid
down by the Law for the Organisation of National
Labour of January 1934. Its essential principles
are to be seen clearly in the first two articles:

Article 1. "In a business undertaking, the employer, as leader, and the employees, as followers,
shall work together to further the purposes of the
undertaking, and for the common good of the
People and of the State."

Article 2. "As between the leader of an undertaking and his followers, the leader shall make
all decisions concerning the undertaking.

"He is to take care of the welfare of the followers. The followers are to keep faith with him in the spirit of solidarity in a joint enterprise."

In general the relations between labour and capital are placed on a unitary basis, in the sense that no scope is allowed for collective negotiations between bodies of workers and bodies of employers, but only between the individual employer and his own workers. Further, the relationship itself is governed by the "leadership principle"; throughout the Law the employer is called the leader and the employees his followers. The significance of this change of terminology and of the ideas behind it is well brought out in the following extract from an important and too little known book (*The Fascist. His State and his Mind*, by E. B. Ashton, Putnam, 1937):

The Germans refuse to admit, on principle, that there is such a thing as an inherent conflict of interest between capital and labour. They consider every single business enterprise as an organic whole—a live particle of the economic body of the nation. Within these micro-organisms hierarchic functions are distributed; the employers are to lead, the workers are to follow.

This new scheme of labour relations, however, is not meant to enlarge any rights of employers based upon ownership of capital or means of production. National Socialism, in converting the employer from an "owner" into a "leader" of his business, changed the whole structural position. His business is no longer regarded as a piece of property to be used, within the law, at its owner's pleasure. It becomes a public trust; and in connection with it, the employer has no longer any *rights* as an independent economic individual and master of his property—he has only state-conferred *powers* which are necessary for the performance of his organic *function*. This function, chiefly, imposes upon him definite and original duties; the duties of the *primus inter pares*—to lead for the good of the whole, to place, in the exercise of the authority which his followers are to obey, the "common good" above his "individual good". As in every other field, the "leadership principle" in economics represents not a superiority of the leader over his followers, but a division of functions between essentially equal parts, with mutual obligations to be discharged in the interest of the collective body.

In place of the former Works Councils, a "Confidential Council" (*Vertrauensrat*) is set up in every undertaking with more than twenty employees. The members of the Council, who must be over 25 years of age, have had a certain minimum period of employment in the undertaking and the industry, be members of the Labour Front, and have an unimpeachable political outlook, are elected by the employees from a list of suitable persons drawn up by the employer. In contrast to the Works Councils Act of 1920 which stated that the Works Councils should "represent the special interests

of the employees as against those of the employer",
the main duty of the members of the Confidential
Council is to "deepen the mutual confidence that
must exist within the works community (*Betriebs-
gemeinschaft*)".

Another difference consists in the fact that the
Confidential Councils, like the works committees
set up in this country under the Whitley scheme,
can only operate in conjunction with the employer,
who is himself a member of the Council instead
of being an external authority with whom it has
to negotiate. The Confidential Councils have also
to co-operate in increasing efficiency, in the draw-
ing up of works rules, and in the maintenance of
friendly and peaceful relations in the undertaking,
and so on. The Law provides for the annual
election of the Confidential Councillors by secret
ballot, but it is noteworthy that the last election
took place in the spring of 1935, and that since
that date the tenure of those holding office has
been prolonged from year to year without any
fresh election being held. The natural interpretation which would come immediately to the mind
of the citizen of a Western democratic State is that
the authorities have been afraid to trust to the
results of a new election. This may well be so,
but as the lists are in any case drawn up by the
employer, it is possible that the decision to

prolong the tenure was also partly influenced by the
fact that employers as a whole were satisfied with
the composition of the councils by 1935, and did
not want to lose the experience and knowledge
acquired by the existing members. In any event
the holding of annual elections is not consistent
with the leadership principle which, as has already
been pointed out, is a cardinal feature of the Nazi
State, and it is scarcely surprising that it should
have been dropped.[1] Whether the satisfaction of
the employers with the composition and co-
operation of the Councils is also shared by the
employees themselves, whom these Councils are
deemed to represent, but upon whom they are in
fact imposed, is a very relevant and important
question, but it is one to which unfortunately no
answer can be given on any broad basis of ascer-
tained fact. Even a provisional or partial con-
clusion could probably only be drawn by one who
had had access to the files of the Labour Front
and of the Trustees of Labour. Any direct
investigation among the workers would clearly
be impracticable owing to the ever-present fear of
reprisals. In this respect the situation is similar

[1] A Law of 1 April 1938 prolonged the appointment of
Confidential Councillors for an indefinite period. In future the
Trustees of Labour were to be responsible for filling any
vacancies in existing Councils and for appointing Confidential
Councillors in new undertakings.

to that prevailing in Soviet Russia, but neither in the case of Germany nor in that of Russia would it be safe to assume from this fact that a large majority of the workers would *necessarily* be found more hostile to their working conditions, if they felt completely free to express their real sentiments, than the workers in other industrial countries.

A very important role in the shaping of industrial relations is played by the Trustees of Labour (*Treuhänder der Arbeit*). These are Federal officials who are appointed for each of the main economic districts into which Germany is divided (seventeen in number) and who are subject to the authority of the Minister of Labour. Whereas all individual disputes, e.g. as to the wages to which an individual worker is entitled, are decided as in the past by the Labour Courts, disputes between the workers of an undertaking as a body and the employer, or between a majority of the workers' representatives on the Confidential Council and the employer, are decided by the Trustees of Labour. It is their principal task to preserve social and economic peace, and they have very extensive powers. Thus if the Trustee is of opinion that a decision by the employer affecting the well-being of the workers is unjustified, he has the power to cancel it, and impose his own ruling on the employer.

In every factory or other business with twenty or more employees a set of works rules (*Betriebs-ordnung*) containing provisions regulating working hours, piece-work remuneration, penalties, grounds for dismissal, holidays, etc., must be drawn up in collaboration with the Confidential Council and posted. It is the duty of the Trustee of Labour to supervise the framing and execution of these rules and to intervene when they run contrary to general policy. If a majority of the Confidential Council disagrees with the draft rules presented by the employer, and no agreement can be reached, the Trustee himself issues the rules.

The intention of the National Labour Law and the influence exerted by the Labour Trustees, at any rate during the first five years of the régime, was that works rules should be as favourable to the workers as the conditions would allow, and as far as possible more favourable than the type of rules which had prevailed during the Weimar Republic. From 1935 onwards this tendency was strengthened by the widespread competition for the designation of "model business",[1] in the granting of which the nature of the works rules was one of the relevant considerations. If it is merely assumed that the winning over of the mass

[1] See below, pp. 41–2.

of German labour to the Nazi cause was of vital moment to the party, this policy can be readily understood.

One of the directions in which the new works rules were most conspicuously in advance of those earlier in force consisted in the provisions for holidays with pay. In all the main industries where a collective regulation embodying holidays with pay is in force (this is the general rule) corresponding provisions must be inserted in the works rules. Where no general regulation can be made the individual firms are encouraged to draw up their own schemes, and in many of the larger concerns additional schemes for supplementing the officially recognised payments, or the duration of the holiday period, are operated on a contributory basis within the works.

In practice the most important of the functions of the Trustees of Labour has to do with the issue of collective regulations governing wages, hours, and working conditions over the greater part of industry. It was laid down in principle by the National Labour Law that wages and other conditions of work should be determined separately for each undertaking. The obvious danger then arose that the whole wage structure of the country would be thrown into confusion, and that chaos would result. Accordingly the Law stated that all collective agreements (*Tarifverträge*) in force on 30 April 1934 should remain for the time being unaltered, but the Trustees of Labour were given power to replace these collective agreements by collective regulations (*Tarifordnungen*). The essential difference in principle between the *Tarifvertrag* and the *Tarifordnung* lay in the fact that the former, at least in origin, was a negotiated settlement, while the latter was a settlement imposed on both parties by a State official, without there being any possibility of recourse to either a strike or a lock-out. Extensive use has been made of these powers and over 2000 major collective regulations were issued between 1934 and the end of 1937.

Whenever the provisions of a collective regulation differed from those of the works rules of an undertaking, it was the former which were to have priority over the latter, in so far as they were more favourable to the workers. This latter proviso held good broadly until July 1938, but from then onwards the over-riding power of the Trustees was used increasingly to lengthen hours of work above all in the munitions industries, to hold wages in check, and, after the outbreak of the war, even to reduce earnings, abrogate holidays with pay, etc.[1]

Holidays with pay (combined with the cheap

[1] See below, pp. 73-4.

travel service of *Kraft durch Freude*) have in fact been one of the most popular developments under the aegis of the Nazi régime. They existed fairly widely before 1933, but the big expansion came, as in most other countries, after that date. In Germany holidays with pay were embodied in the collective regulations issued by the Trustees of Labour for almost all industries, and much ingenuity was expended in devising practicable schemes even in such cases as the building industry, with its seasonal and migratory employment, and in agriculture and forestry. The duration of holidays with pay is graded according to the number of years' service of the employee in question and in 1934 ranged on an average from a minimum of five to a maximum of eleven days, in the chemical industries the maximum being sixteen days. The average duration for juveniles has normally been made considerably longer than for adults; thus in the building trades, where it ranged from four to six days for adults, the corresponding period for juveniles was eight to twelve days, but in most industries the difference was not so great as this. The general tendency from 1934 down to September 1939 was in the direction of widening the scope and increasing the duration of holidays with pay.

The wage policy of the Trustees of Labour

throughout the period down to 1939 has been dominated by the general principles underlying the economic policy of the State, which may be expressed in the phrase: stable wages and stable prices. The new collective regulations maintained intact the general level of minimum wage rates established by the former collective agreements, but certain specially low wages, e.g. in certain branches of the building and constructional industries, were raised, and steps were taken to remove all sorts of regional and local anomalies which had arisen under the earlier system.

"The collective regulation constitutes the formative law of German labour. Administered centrally by the State and not by the interests concerned, it provides the touchstone for policy. Its elasticity affords a testing period during which what is practicable can be tried out before it is finally incorporated in statutory form. Thus questions of hours of work, rates and periods of remuneration, local variations, demarcation questions, holidays, periods for notice of dismissal, etc., can be examined and decided in accordance with the principle of 'Service to the German people'. The harmful conflicts between different German economic areas can be avoided, the question of the localisation of undertakings can be separated from the wage problem and approximately equal conditions in respect of labour cost can be assured."[1]

The foregoing passage is cited not as providing any direct evidence of fact, but as showing the direction in which supporters of the system of the authoritarian regulation of wages look for its advantages and merits.

Although the policy of stabilisation of minimum wage rates has been strictly adhered to, there was in fact a considerable rise in earnings. Thus in the period from 1933 to the beginning of 1938, average hourly earnings of industrial workers in the most important industries of the country rose by 10 % and average weekly earnings by 20 %. During the same period the cost of living index number showed an increase of 6 %, though the real increase in the cost of living was rather greater than this owing to changes in quality. This increase in earnings was due to such factors as the wider adoption of piece-wages, promotions to higher wage scales, longer hours of work, payments for holidays, and higher wages offered to attract or retain labour.

Prior to July 1938, apart from restrictions on the "poaching" of individual workers in the building and engineering industries, there was no

[1] O. Mönckmeier, *Jahrbuch der National-Sozialistischen Wirtschaft*, 1937, p. 63.

interference with the right of the employer to pay to any category of labour wages which were higher than the minimum wage rates laid down in the collective regulation. But in 1938, under the stress of the foreign reaction to the seizure of Austria, and of the building of the Siegfried Line in the West, powers were given to the Labour Trustees to control all wage movements, the intention being that they should prevent rises in wages which were merely due to increasing scarcity of labour coupled with ever-increasing industrial activity. Higher earnings which were the result of greater efficiency were, however, to continue.

With the outbreak of the war in September 1939 the Trustees of Labour were ordered to "adjust earnings to the conditions entailed by the war and to lay down, by collective regulations, binding wages, salaries and other conditions of work, with a maximum level".[1] The Trustees were now in a position, not merely to prevent any increases of wages, but to lower existing efficiency bonuses if they considered them too high; they were also empowered to issue collective regulations to apply to a single undertaking. In place of the old

[1] The over-riding of all the provisions contained in the collective regulations for overtime pay in respect of hours in excess of the normal, and of Sunday and night work, as well as for holidays with pay, is noted below, pp. 73–4.

minimum rates of wages (including piece rates) they could now fix maximum earnings, and in certain cases they used their powers to reduce the previous level of wages. By a Decree of 12 October 1939, employers were forbidden in general to raise existing wage or salary rates or any other form of regular remuneration, or to increase the workers' earnings by means of non-recurrent allowances. It was further decreed that established piece-work rates (including bonuses) might not, except by specific authorisation of a Trustee of Labour, be altered for the purpose of increasing earnings, while new rates must be carefully fixed in such a way that earnings should not exceed those customary in the undertaking for the class of work in question. The Decree also prohibited the reduction of wages, salaries and allowances, under the same conditions and subject to the same reservations as those governing the raising of wages. However, reductions might be authorised or approved by a Trustee of Labour in cases where the earnings were not directly related to output.

Two other provisions of the National Labour Law remain to be mentioned—the Courts of Social Honour, and the protection against unjustified dismissal.

In each of the seventeen economic districts into

which Germany has been divided, a Court of Social Honour is established, as well as a Federal Court in Berlin to act as an appeal tribunal. Each Court consists of a judge, an employer and a Confidential Councillor. The Court hears charges brought either against employers or employees of gross offences against the social obligations inherent in the concept of the works community. Thus a Confidential Councillor or other worker who has been false to his trust by betraying secrets of the firm or by some other flagrant act of disloyalty, or the employer who insults the honour of an employee, may be summoned before the Court and reprimanded or fined or dismissed. The Trustee of Labour acts as prosecutor, and is responsible for bringing the case to Court, and he will as a rule issue warnings before taking action. Hence the number of cases each year has been few; most of the defendants have been employers and in a few instances the most drastic penalty, that of dismissal from his position as employer (*Betriebsführer*), has been imposed. When regard is had to the temperamental nature of the Germans and to the characteristics of a certain type of employer, the *raison d'être* of this novel institution and its potential value as an influence restraining the arbitrary abuse of the employers' power can be realised. How effective it has proved in fact it is impossible to say, and the small number of the cases would appear to point to its being more a façade than a reality. On the other hand, officials in the office of the Labour Trustee in Hamburg, with whom the writer spoke in 1938, declared that the existence of the Court was of genuine value, and that a large number of cases was dealt with by the Trustees by way of warning and admonition, which never came before the Court.

Finally the Law provides that in undertakings with ten or more employees a worker who has had not less than one year's service with the firm can appeal to the Labour Court against his dismissal on the ground that it was unjust and not rendered necessary by the economic conditions of the business. If the Labour Court upholds the appeal and the employer is not willing to take the man back, the Court determines the amount of compensation to be paid to the worker; this normally may not exceed one-half of the income earned by the worker during the year immediately preceding his dismissal, but in exceptional cases the employer may be ordered to pay compensation equal to the amount earned by the worker during the whole year. An example of this occurred in 1937 when a worker at Gelsenkirchen, who had had twenty years' service with a firm, was dismissed "without due cause" and was awarded by the Court the amount of his previous year's earnings as compensation.

THE LABOUR FRONT

The German Labour Front is in no sense a part of the machinery of the State and it is not subordinate to the Ministry of Labour. It is an organ of the Nazi Party and has behind it all the power and authority of the party. Its main function is to reconcile the vast body of German workers of every grade with the social and political aims of the Nazi régime—by no means a simple task when it is remembered that by the beginning of 1933 a large part of German labour, especially the younger section, had fallen under the sway of communist doctrines.

In principle, membership of the Labour Front is voluntary, but in practice, except for Jews who may not belong to it, virtually the whole of German workers, and nearly all German employers, are members. The workers pay on the average a contribution of 1·6 marks per month and the employers a contribution based on the size of the undertaking. As the Labour Front has a membership of over twenty-five millions, and as it had taken over all the accumulated funds of the old trade unions, it can be seen that its financial resources are very great; in 1937 its revenue was

360 million marks. It enjoys therefore both immense political power and immense wealth.

On the one hand the Labour Front holds a watching brief in everything that concerns industrial relations, while on the other it carries out multifarious activities of the most diverse kind with a view to convincing German Labour that the Nazi Party has above all the welfare of the workers at heart.

In the first of these capacities the Labour Front seeks to maintain industrial peace and to conciliate differences if possible before they reach the stage of reference to a Labour Trustee or a Labour Court for an arbitral award. It is in a position to bring, and does in fact bring, great pressure to bear on employers to concede what it considers to be the just claims of the workers. It is true of course that the Labour Front, unlike the trade unions which it has replaced, is not a workers' organisation; its officials are appointed by the Party, and its membership includes employers as well as employees. It is also expressly forbidden to intervene directly in the determination of wages, which is the province of the Trustees of Labour, but the nature of its personnel and its whole structure and function as an organ of the Nazi *Party* results in a bias which it is said tends to be more pro-worker than pro-employer. The head of the Labour Front,

Dr Ley, represents the moderate Left Wing of the Party, and his influence has been a dominating factor in moulding its practical policy. At the same time it is important to recognise that the fundamental bias of the Labour Front is pro-Party, and that every other consideration yields place to what may be called the "Party Line".[1] If the Party Line, as in war time or in immediate preparation for war, involves longer hours or a deterioration in working conditions, including wages, then the whole machinery of the Labour Front will be directed to persuade the workers of the necessity of these measures and of their patriotic duty as members of the folk community (*Volksgemein-schaft*) to accept loyally any sacrifices which the national emergency is held to require.

In its second main capacity the Labour Front pursues with remarkable success the policy of *panem et circenses*, though the emphasis is more on the circuses than the bread. Its most spectacular activity is *Kraft durch Freude* (Strength through Joy). This is an organisation on a grandiose scale (the idea was copied from the Italian *Dopolavoro*), for bringing holiday travel, recreation and sport within the range of the masses of the population. In the years 1936 to 1938 over six million persons

[1] Here as in other cases the parallel with Soviet Russian para-State institutions (cf. the trade unions) is very close.

annually took part in holiday trips, many of them
for long distances and at only a fraction of the
normal cost. Special *Kraft durch Freude* ships were
built and holiday cruises arranged in the Baltic
and Mediterranean, though the number taking
part in these was naturally relatively small (180,000
in 1938). Nor were the participants by any means
confined to those who were loudest in their
support of the régime. It was a carefully thought-
out part of the plan to include, *inter alia,* ex-
communists who had been known locally for their
extreme views or who were believed to be dis-
contented, and to send them along too on some
of the most attractive tours. As a skilfully devised
propaganda plays a large role in all the *Kraft durch
Freude* activities, the cumulative effect of these
trips, which coincided with a great extension of
holidays with pay, must have been very considerable. In addition to travel, *Kraft durch Freude*
organised music, theatres, entertainments and
sport for the million. Thus as early as September
1936 it was stated that 52,700,000 had attended
entertainments organised by the entertainment
section of *Kraft durch Freude* during the preceding
two years. Much has been done also, both in the
villages and in the factories, to organise musical
and dramatic activities in which the people themselves could take part. In this connection care

is taken that everything that is done is fitted into
its national environment—the old peasant dresses
are revived, old folk music and dances resuscitated,
and no opportunity is lost of enhancing the
national consciousness and the feeling of pride
in the past achievements of the German people
and of confidence in the possibilities of the future.
Thus (and in many other ways also) it is sought
to wipe out the humiliating memories of the defeat
of 1918 and to restore to the Germans their lost
self-respect.

Like the Japanese, the Nazis are afraid of
"dangerous thoughts" and both on grounds of
physical fitness and as a means of occupying the
leisure time of the workers and diverting their
minds from other preoccupations, they have
thrown themselves with their usual energy and
enthusiasm into the organisation of sport on mass
production lines. Thus Dr Ley has stated that
in 1936 six million persons took part in sporting
arrangements organised by *Kraft durch Freude*, and
that 2800 whole-time sporting instructors were
being maintained.

Further there is an important branch of *Kraft
durch Freude* entitled *Schönheit der Arbeit* (Beauty
of Work), which is concerned with improving
the amenities of life of the worker. Inspectors
are sent into the factories and many hundreds of

them are visited annually. Wherever the canteen arrangements are missing or are ugly, dirty or dark, the employer is told that he must make the necessary improvements and he is "encouraged" to make other improvements, e.g. in matters of lighting and ventilation, washing and dressing rooms, etc.; the "encouragement" is apt to be somewhat dictatorial and a failure to acquiesce in the suggestion of the inspectors is effectively "discouraged". It is estimated that in 1936 and 1937 employers were induced to spend some 300 million marks per annum on improvements to their premises as a result of the activities of this section of the Labour Front, while large sums were also contributed out of the funds of the Labour Front itself.

In order to stimulate not only this type of improvement but every sort of provision for the comfort and well-being of the workers, there has been since 1936 an annual competition for the honour of being designated a "model business" (*Musterbetrieb*), i.e. a concern which has reached the highest standard in its provision for the welfare of its employees. Those who gain this distinction (the number is deliberately kept quite small) are allowed to display a special token on their works and on their notepaper; it is an honour which is greatly prized on general grounds and which, from an advertising point of view, brings with it some solid economic advantages. It has also been shown that the efficiency of labour and with it the level of earnings of the workers has increased in those undertakings which have taken part in the contests.[1] In the early summer of 1938 as many as 84,000 businesses competed for this honour and they were able to prove that they had expended voluntarily 786 million RM. in welfare schemes, housing, etc., on behalf of their employees. One hundred and two firms in all had gained the distinction by May 1938. The adjudicators are said to have the four following points chiefly in mind: (1) the maintenance and safeguarding of social peace; (2) the maintenance and increase of the strength of the people (*Volkskraft*); (3) the maintenance and increase of the power of work and the raising of the standard of living; (4) economic policy in the light of the aims of political leadership. In addition, diplomas are given in rather larger numbers for outstanding achievements in individual directions, such as training and apprenticeship, provision of workers' dwell-

---

[1] The writer has come across a complaint that, in their eagerness to get the title of model business, some firms have driven their workers extra hard, so as to show as high a labour efficiency in terms of output as possible. But he is not aware of any evidence whether this has taken place, or, if true, how general it is.

ings, hygiene, support of *Kraft durch Freude*, etc. All these competitions are still being maintained during the present war.

Besides all these activities, the Labour Front is also closely concerned with the position of the independent craftsman (*Handwerker*), with the relief of distress, and with the housing and training of the workers. These will be discussed in later chapters. But it also itself conducts undertakings on a considerable scale. Thus the People's Car works at Fallersleben is a Labour Front enterprise; and the Front also administers the Labour Bank, an important life insurance concern, a building undertaking, a large publishing business, and so on.

Chapter III

EMPLOYMENT POLICY

The Conquest of Unemployment

THE great world economic depression of 1930–32 had struck Germany with special violence. Her industries were largely paralysed, her banking system broke down completely in the summer of 1931 and became unable to extend further credits to industry; the long-term rate of interest was over 7 %; savings were a negative amount, and the capital market had entirely ceased to function. When Hitler came into power on 30 January 1933, there were more than six million unemployed, which meant that at least one-third of the German working population was out of work. It was this economic blizzard which—as we have already stated in Chapter I—was mainly responsible for the overthrow of the Weimar Republic and its replacement by the National Socialist State. Hitler promised the German people what at that time seemed the greatest boon of all—employment.

In May 1933 he put forward his first Four Year Plan for the conquest of unemployment. In the Plan he attacked the problem not only from one, but from many different angles. In the first place, taking over the financial technique already worked out under von Papen, he drew up vast programmes of capital expenditure on roads, canals, housing, land improvement, railways, etc., which were financed neither by loans nor by taxes, but by the creation of central bank credit. Secondly, women were withdrawn as far as possible from employment, so that their places could be taken by men. To facilitate this, marriage loans up to £50 were given to women who got married, on condition that they gave up their jobs.

Thirdly, subsidies were given on a large scale for house repairs and improvements; the motor industry was stimulated by the exemption of new motor cars from taxation; profits spent on renewal or replacement of plant were also exempted from taxation and so on.

Fourthly, there was a great increase in "substitute employment", chiefly in the form of relief works. This consisted of all sorts of public works, mostly of an unskilled character, which were undertaken largely by municipalities or other local authorities, and on which the unemployed, irrespective of their occupation, were employed. These workers were paid on the lowest scale for unskilled labour, and their earnings were little, if at all, above what they would have otherwise drawn in the form of unemployment allowances. Indeed, a great part of the funds required to finance these relief works came from the Unemployment Insurance Fund, and the same is true of another form of substitute employment—the Labour Service, about which more will be said later. In one month in 1934 the total volume of substitute employment rose to over one million.

Lastly, hours of work were reduced, so as to spread employment, corresponding reductions being made in earnings, and employers were severely restricted in their power to dismiss their workers. It is true that this helped to diminish unemployment, but at the cost of a serious reduction in the general level of earnings.

The net result of all these measures, combined with the general forces making for economic recovery, was that unemployment fell from six millions at the beginning of 1933 to 2·6 millions in December 1934.

Early in 1935 Germany left the Disarmament Conference and started rearming on an enormous scale, just at the moment when the employment programmes of 1933 were running down, with the exception of the new motor roads, of what might be termed a normal building programme, and of a certain amount of work on the canals. With the other features of Germany's economic revival—the expansion of the national income and of savings, the reduction of the rate of interest, the restoration of the capital market, there is no space to deal here.[1] It must suffice to say that by September 1936 unemployment had fallen to one million, of which 500,000 might be said to be a "normal" minimum for an industrial country of the size of Germany. Hitler could contend, therefore, that the Four Year Plan had succeeded in its objects and that unemployment had been largely conquered; though it is important to recognise that since the end of 1934 it was rearmament which had played the chief role in the absorption of the unemployed.

At the same time as this industrial recovery was proceeding, drastic changes were being made in agriculture. In the first place, the whole of agricultural marketing was reorganised and placed under central control and direction; secondly, prices of agricultural products were initially raised and then stabilised for at least one year ahead and were removed from the fluctuations of the world market; thirdly, peasant farms up to a maximum of 309 acres were declared "hereditary farms" which were entailed in perpetuity and could neither be sold nor mortgaged. By these measures the very

[1] For a full account see C. W. Guillebaud, *The Economic Recovery of Germany*, 1933 *to* 1938.

important agricultural section of the country was effectively appeased, at any rate for the time being, and, despite inevitable frictions and difficulties, was ranged on the whole behind the banner of Hitler.

In September 1936 Hitler announced the Second Four Year Plan to render Germany independent of foreign sources of supply of essential materials and foodstuffs. Rearmament was pushed ahead with redoubled vigour, and an enormous amount of new investment was required for the new "substitute" raw material factories. By the spring of 1938 full employment had been reached in many branches of German industry, and in place of surplus labour there was an acute and growing scarcity of labour, above all in the constructional and engineering industries.

Having reached this point, we may pause to consider for a moment the general attitude of the National Socialist Party towards the problem of unemployment. The "right to work" is a cardinal feature of their economic policy. This implies, on the one hand the recognition of the fact that the State is responsible for providing work rather than maintenance, for those who are unable to obtain work in their normal occupations; but on the other hand it also implies equally strongly the doctrine of the "duty of work"—the obligation of the worker to accept work under the conditions and in the locality where it is offered, even though it may be different work and in a different locality from that in which he ordinarily lives.

Now it is beyond question true that the largest part of the hold which the National Socialist régime has acquired amongst the masses, the most important cause of that general contentment of which Mr de Courcy has spoken,[1] is due to the abolition of unemployment. After the devastating experience of 1930–33, the German worker could feel—at any rate down to September 1939—that he had been given economic security, and no longer need fear widespread involuntary unemployment. That the method by which this result has been partly, though by no means wholly, brought about—intensive rearmament—is an abnormal one, and that some day a testing time must arrive when swords will again be beaten into ploughshares, is no doubt true; but the worker has faith in the organising powers of his Government, and a belief in the reality of the State recognition of the right to work, which has been drilled into him by a never-ceasing propaganda. In the meantime he enjoys economic security, in the sense that he feels that his job, or if not his job, then a job, is secure. Moreover, he knows that the continuity

[1] See p. iv of this book.

of his employment is in no danger of being inter-
rupted by either a strike or a lock-out. It is true
that a short stoppage of work, in the type of
industry where employment is normally continuous, may even be welcome to the workers
(apart from the merits of the case) since it means
a change and a period of rest,[1] but a long-drawn-out
industrial dispute with no unemployment pay—
except for the trade union's limited strike benefits
—will result in very real hardship for the families
of the strikers. This is a contingency against which
State insurance schemes do not, and cannot, provide. It must also be borne in mind that by no
means all of those who are thrown out of work by
a strike, or suffer through it, are willing parties
to the dispute. While the prohibition of the right
to strike is beyond doubt a serious interference
with the freedom of action of the workers and
deprives them of their most powerful ultimate
weapon against the employer, it does bring with
it an added feeling of security which is at least
a partial set-off against the forfeiture of this
weapon. In fact, if employment is good and real
wages are not falling, the workers and their
families may be more conscious of this greater

[1] From this point of view, the general extension of holidays
with pay in Germany since 1933 may be regarded as a corollary
of the abolition of the right to strike.

security than they are of their lost industrial liberties.[1]

When, however, German labour policy is viewed from a wider standpoint than that of its immediate effect on the workers themselves, it is clear that the latter have forfeited the right to share in the determination of their own wages and working conditions. They are the passive objects of decisions in which they have had no voice; and though there may be a gain in efficiency and in the smooth running of the industrial system, there is a very great offset which must be put against this for the loss which it entails of freedom—freedom to co-operate, to learn by mistakes, to acquire a sense of responsibility, and thereby to build up eventually the structure of a free society.

In the later period, to which after this digression we now return, the emphasis on the "duty to work" was no longer to be found in the alternative between any form of work and maintenance, but in the obligation of the worker to do the kind of work that was assigned to him by the State.[2] From the inception of the Second Four Year Plan in

[1] This, and the foregoing sentences, must not be interpreted as a plea for abolishing the right to strike, but as a possible explanation why the German workers, or large numbers of them, may not regard its abolition as an *unmixed* evil.

[2] It should be noted that substitute employment diminished rapidly in 1935, and (except for the Labour Service) became negligible in the later years.

September 1936 onwards the great slogan was *Arbeitseinsatz*, or the most effective utilisation of the available (scarce) labour force of the country.

Already quite early on the State had interfered (rather ineffectively) in special cases with freedom of movement or the choice of occupation. An Act of 12 May 1934 had empowered steps to be taken to check the flight of labour from the land and prevent the migration of workers from the country districts to certain areas such as Berlin and Hamburg. Later with the growing scarcity, especially of skilled labour, more and more power was given to the Employment Exchanges to control the flow of labour. An important role in the control is played by the Employment Book, which, since February 1935, every German wage earner or salaried employee is compelled to keep. In this book is recorded his training and the different jobs he has held, so that it gives a record of his whole industrial career.

In November 1936, among other decrees issued by Field-Marshal Göring as Commissioner for the Second Four Year Plan, was one requiring the approval of the Employment Exchanges when any employer took on ten or more additional workers in the metal industries, and in May 1938 it applied also to the building and constructional trades. This was no mere formality, but was accompanied by a close scrutiny of the extent to which the employer in question was making the best use of the labour force already at his disposal.

Taking the field of employment as a whole, however, and even including these specially regulated industries, there were no serious restrictions prior to 1938 on the right of the worker to leave his job and go elsewhere if he thought he could better his position. It is true that in the building and metal trades the employer was not allowed to tempt individual workers away from another employer in the same trade by the offer of higher wages; but he could offer higher wages all round to all his workers and so improve his position in the labour market. There was in fact a tremendous amount of labour transfer of all kinds throughout this period, not least in connection with the construction of the new raw material factories built under the Second Four Year Plan, and some of this was of a type definitely unwelcome to the National Socialist authorities. Thus by the autumn of 1938 the loss of agricultural labour due to its migration into other occupations was officially estimated at over 700,000 in comparison with 1933.

A dramatic interference with freedom of labour took place in the summer of 1938, when the Siegfried Line was constructed. Hundreds of thousands of men were drafted away from their homes and usual occupations and sent to Western Germany. This measure, a veritable conscription of labour for a limited period, aroused a great deal of discontent, even though the wages were the same as the men had previously received. It appears indeed that a minor though none the less highly unpleasant method of punishing refractory workers was to have them sent to work on the Western fortifications.

International tension continued to increase during the remainder of 1938, and in the spring of 1939—coinciding with the seizure of Czecho-Slovakia—the control of labour was put completely on to a war basis. Decrees were then issued which vested the Ministry of Labour with virtually unlimited powers over the supply and disposition of the labour market.

In the first place the Minister of Labour was authorised to call upon the services of any inhabitant of the German Reich for work of special national importance and urgency, and firms and offices could be required to release employees for such services. Henceforward the Employment Exchanges were in a position to requisition or conscript labour for work in other factories and in other branches of industry than those in which the workers were hitherto employed. If, as a result of their previous training in one field, they were not able to accomplish the new type of work, they could be compelled to undergo special training. This measure has in fact been applied on a large scale since the war in the case of textile and other workers, who have been sent for training in the metal industries.

Secondly, the Minister of Labour was empowered to make the termination of labour contracts dependent upon the consent of the Employment Exchanges, and this power was at first applied to the following branches of production: agriculture, forestry, mining (other than hard coal mining), chemicals, building materials, iron and other metals. The consent, however, was not required when both employer and worker were agreed upon termination.

Thirdly, power was given to require the consent of the Employment Exchanges before new contracts were entered into, and this also was applied to the six branches of production mentioned above. Finally, on 1 September 1939 the second and third of these provisions was made applicable to *all* manual and non-manual workers, including domestic servants and apprentices. Henceforward no German worker could change his job without obtaining permission, while if he absented himself from work without proper excuse he was liable to imprisonment.

During 1938–39, when repeated mobilisations and the increase in the numbers of the armed forces had further depleted the supply of labour, steps were taken to comb out workers from occupations that were regarded as overstocked or superfluous. Surveys were made of hairdressing establishments, small shopkeepers, and other independent craftsmen, and their businesses were closed down if it was held that their continued existence had no economic justification. By these and other measures labour was drawn into employment to a far greater degree than corresponded to the decline in unemployment. Thus between April 1938 and April 1939 employment rose by 1,309,000, while unemployment declined only from 423,000 to 94,000.

A notable feature of the later German employment policy has been the reintroduction of women into industry and other occupations. In the early stages much play was made with such ideas as that women's place was in the home, and that factory employment was detrimental to marriage, the birthrate and infantile mortality; but as labour grew more scarce these ideas fell into the background, and instead every effort was made to attract women back into employment. Thus the number of employed women increased from 4·7 millions in 1933 to 6·3 millions in 1938,[1] and there was a further expansion in 1939. An

[1] Proportionately, however, women's employment expanded less than that of men—nine million men in 1933 and thirteen million in 1938.

interesting decree of February 1938, applying to certain categories of women, was influenced partly by social considerations and partly by the general labour situation: in future no unmarried girl or woman under twenty-five years of age, coming new into the labour market, could obtain employment in any commercial capacity, or as a worker in the clothing, textile or tobacco industries, unless she could show that she had previously spent one year working on the land or in domestic service, or two years as an auxiliary nurse or social welfare worker; and in December 1938 this was extended to cover entry into all private or public undertakings.

When the later employment policy of Germany, especially in the years 1938–39, is considered as a whole, it is clear that it involved very serious encroachments on the freedom of action of the workers (the same statement could be equally made, though with a different significance, in regard to the employers). The workers have found themselves constrained to work longer hours in many cases than they would have done voluntarily; in the face of an extreme scarcity of labour their wage rates have been prevented from rising; and their right (in some cases) to choose their own employment and even their own occupation has been restricted. Nevertheless, it must not be forgotten that the more drastic of these encroachments were undertaken, not because they were regarded as desirable in themselves—this would be the reverse of the truth—but because they were regarded as necessary defence (or offence) measures resulting from a national emergency. Given Hitler's foreign policy, the external reactions to it were clearly such as to call for abnormal measures in many fields, including that of labour policy. The fact that these resulted in a diminution of economic welfare was, from the Nazi point of view, a regrettable but unavoidable short-run consequence of the course of action in foreign affairs to which the German people had been committed by Hitler's leadership.

THE TRAINING OF LABOUR

A very important aspect of employment policy, and one to which the Nazis have paid much attention, is the training and occupational guidance of the young. As a result of the depression of 1930–32, there had been a great decline in the number of apprentices and learners in the skilled trades, which gave rise to anxiety for the future. Hence one of the main duties with which the Labour Front was charged from the outset was that of the training of labour. An enormous activity has in fact been developed in this field. In every town and village training schemes have

been organised and courses given. By September
1939 the Labour Front alone had 16,000 full-time
practical instructors for training courses. From
1936 onwards competitions have been held
throughout the country. With the aid of an army
of voluntary workers candidates are tested by
both theoretical and practical examinations. In
1937–39 some two million persons took part in
this examination. The winners in the village would
go on to compete in their district, those from the
district to the province, until, in the last stage of
the weeding-out process some six thousand would
meet in a German city for the final test. Of these
some three or four hundred would be selected as
the winners (*Reichssieger*). These are a sort of
German equivalent of the Russian *Stakhanovists*,
though the proof of distinction is not the same
in the two cases, but they are equally sure of
advancement and reward. Many of the better
qualified of those eliminated in the earlier rounds
of this vast competition are also marked out for
special consideration and assistance. In 1938 it
was stated that out of the 6500 regional winners
63 % received special help and further training
as having demonstrated their particular quality.
It has been the aim of those at the head of the
Labour Front that no one of real capacity throughout Germany shall fail to get his chance of bettering

his position for lack of opportunity or want of money—no one, that is, who besides working capacity also satisfies the political requirements of the Nazi régime. The ex-communist house painter, who described National Socialism as a movement which would enable him to meet his employer outside working hours on an equal basis while allowing himself, if he had the ability, to work himself out of the ruck for the benefit of future members of his family, was expressing an attitude towards the régime which is by no means devoid of significance.

Apart from the activities of the Labour Front the main form of training of skilled labour consists of various types of apprenticeship and learner systems in the factories themselves. In addition to these, all the various forms of handicrafts require several years of apprenticeship ending in a stiff professional examination, which must be passed before a man can be recognised as a master craftsman.

Training schemes inside the factory were encouraged as much as possible by the Labour Front and were made one of the criteria for success in the annual competitions for the distinction of being recognised as a "model business". The training bench or shop is now an established and important feature of almost all engineering works.

But the first direct State intervention of importance took place in November 1936 when it was laid down in the first of the Decrees issued in connection with the Second Four Year Plan, that employers in all undertakings in the iron and metal and the constructional industries employing ten or more workers, must take on apprentices in an appropriate proportion to the number of their skilled workers. The President of the National Labour Board was empowered to determine in each case what the appropriate proportion should be. If any employer could show that he was not in a position to fulfil this requirement, he must make a corresponding payment to the Labour Board towards the annual costs of training. The result of this measure was that the number of apprenticeship and learner posts offered in the iron and metal industries rose from 91,000 in 1935–36 to 126,000 in 1936–37, and those in the constructional trades from 30,300 to 44,600.

With the inauguration of the Second Four Year Plan and the ever-increasing scarcity of skilled labour, training became the rage, and the Group of Industry (*Reichsgruppe Industrie*) recognised officially large numbers of new grades of skilled occupations, each of which had its apprenticeship period of three or four years and its special examination.

Abuses inevitably crept in, as many people were quite unfitted to train apprentices; hence early in 1938 it was found necessary to require the sanction of the Employment Exchange before any person or firm could take on an apprentice.

At about the same time, though for quite different reasons, all children leaving school, whether elementary or secondary, were required to register with the Employment Exchanges, which thus gained a complete survey of the whole youth of the country and of the occupations into which it was going. Previously the Exchanges had cognisance of those children only who had registered with them for jobs. In this connection it is of interest to note that in 1935 the National Labour Board (of which the Employment Exchanges are the local machinery) was given the monopoly of all employment agency work and of vocational guidance. The few non-official agencies which are allowed to exist have to work with the licence and under the direction of the Board. Great importance is attached to vocational guidance, and efforts are made to forecast the future demand for the different occupations and to guide applicants accordingly.

In July 1938 a new School Law for the Reich was enacted, which provided for universal compulsory vocational training after the end of the

normal compulsory school period. For agricultural occupation the minimum duration of
compulsory training is two years and for all other
occupations three years. Only those going to the
universities or to other higher types of education
are exempted. But owing to the scarcity of com-
petent teachers the prospective value of some at
least of the training thus provided was distinctly
doubtful. As the German paper *Die Deutsche
Volkswirtschaft* observed in this connection, it is
not much good for an intending butcher to be
taught by a baker, or for a metal machinist to
receive instruction from a woodworker.

A change of some importance was made in
October 1938 when the duration of apprenticeship
was reduced, by amounts ranging from six months
to eighteen months, to a uniform period of three
years, in order to accelerate the intake of skilled
labour into industry. The standard of the final
examination does not, however, appear to have
been lowered, for in one interesting case which
came before a Labour Court, an apprentice, who
had sought to take advantage of the shortened
course, but who had failed to satisfy the examiners,
brought an action, as by law he was entitled to do,
against his employer on the ground that he had
not received proper instruction. The Court decided against the apprentice, for it held that only

an exceptionally good man could be expected to reach the required standard in the shorter time now allowed, and that the failure of the apprentice was attributable to his own lack of diligence and capacity rather than to any negligence on the part of the employer.

Finally, a brief reference may be made to some post-war developments. On 28 September 1939, a Decree of the new Economic Defence Council made the training of their *unskilled* labour for skilled work a duty incumbent upon all employers in the metal industries. The scheme is based on four weeks' courses of intensive training as the initial stage. The workers trained in these courses are paid during their training time at unskilled rates. After the course they are taken over by a firm and receive further training. Great pressure can be brought to bear upon employers to send their unskilled workers to the officially arranged training courses, because firms which are held not to do enough in that direction can be excluded from any allocation of skilled workers from the Employment Exchanges. On the other hand there is an obligation on employers to accept people trained in these officially approved training courses when they are allocated to them by the Employment Exchange. It is stated that the official training schemes aim generally at devoting 20 %

of the total training time to general instruction, the next 40 % to special training in the job which the trainees are intended to perform, and the remaining 40 % to practical execution of their jobs, with supervision by the instructor, quality tests and gradual speed-up. The real centre of gravity of the scheme lies, however, not in the training courses themselves but in the factories and in the continuation of the training there, especially in the training workshops which are almost universally to be found in engineering factories.

While precise information as to the numbers being trained under these schemes is not available, it is clearly very large, probably of the order of one and a half million per annum or more.

THE COMPULSORY LABOUR SERVICE

The early development of the Labour Service has already been referred to in Chapter 1. Although it remained voluntary, it had already become an official movement by 1931. The Nazis took over the whole institution, and by a Law of 26 June 1935, reorganised it on compulsory lines. Henceforward every young German who was physically fit was to be compelled, in addition to his military service, to spend six months engaged in manual work. The first paragraph of the Law runs as follows: "National Labour Service is a service of honour to the German Reich. All young people of both sexes are obliged to serve their country in the National Labour Service.[1] The function of the Service is to inculcate in the German youth a community spirit and a true concept of the dignity of work, and above all, a proper respect for manual labour. To the National Labour Service is allotted the task of carrying out work for the good of the whole community."

The cost of the scheme is borne by the Reich which allocates 200 million marks out of the budget to cover the whole cost, including administration expenses. Daily board per head is estimated to cost about 85 Pfennigs (about 1s.), and each man receives 25 Pfennigs per day pocket money.

The camps are run on the "leadership principle" and the leader is required to maintain discipline by the exercise of his personal qualities. Punishments of any kind are regarded with disfavour as reflecting adversely on the capacity of the leader to maintain his position. At the same time his authority is no doubt greatly strengthened by the

[1] Hitherto it has only been found possible to apply the law on a small scale to women (the total in 1937 was 15,000 as compared with over 200,000 men). In practice also not all men of the appropriate age groups (18 to 25) have been able to be accommodated in the camps.

fact that each individual is aware that an un-favourable report would be likely to affect adversely his subsequent career and prospects of employment.

In 1937–38 there were some 1300 camps, each containing from 150 to 200 young men who were mainly engaged on work for land reclamation, afforestation, preparing sites for rural settlements and homesteads, road-making in agricultural dis-tricts, and so on. The work is supposed in all cases to be additional to that which would other-wise be undertaken on ordinary financial grounds. In case of emergency those in the Labour Service are available for any kind of work, and they were in fact used extensively in 1938–39 in connection with the construction of the Western fortifications.

The general *social* purpose of the Labour Service has been set out in a speech by Hitler on 1 May 1934, the National Labour Day. "Through the Labour Service we would compel every young German to work at least once with his hands and thus to contribute towards the building up of his people. Above all, we want those Germans who are in sedentary occupations to experience what manual labour is, so that they may feel under-standing and sympathy for those of their country-men whose lives are spent in the fields, the factory or the workshop. We want to abolish for ever that attitude of superiority which unfortunately so many of our intellectuals adopt towards the manual workers, and we wish them to realise that they too will be worth all the more if they know themselves to possess a capacity for physical work. But the ultimate aim behind the Labour Service is to promote mutual understanding between the different classes, and thus to strengthen the spirit of national solidarity among the whole people."

Of all the institutions in Nazi Germany the compulsory Labour Service is the one which has received the widest measure of approval from foreign observers. Perhaps the only substantial criticism that has been urged against it is that the Nazis have partially militarised it, as seems unfortunately to be the case with all the youth organisations in the totalitarian countries. With its quasi-military drill and discipline, and its hardening effects on the physique of the participants, it serves as an effective prelude to the two years of military service which normally follow it. Nevertheless it remains true that the real significance of the compulsory Labour Service in Germany is essentially social rather than military.

Chapter IV

STATE REGULATION OF LABOUR CONDITIONS

Hours of Labour

In the early years of the new régime the National Socialists made few changes in the previous legislation governing hours of work. The Decree of 26 July 1934 was a consolidating measure rather than a new scheme. It maintained the general principle of the eight-hour day (including breaks), but allowed under certain conditions a maximum of ten hours to be worked on any one day. The Decree extended the general provisions regulating hours to transport workers, and raised the age from sixteen to eighteen of young persons not permitted to do Sunday work; this prohibition was also made general instead of, as in the past, applying only to undertakings employing not less than ten persons. In order to give greater elasticity the "double week" of ninety-six hours was introduced and the employer was enabled to distribute the work as he wished within any period of a fortnight, so long as the limit of ninety-six hours in fourteen days was not exceeded.

The actual number of hours worked in most industries was determined by collective regulations issued by the Trustees of Labour, and varied widely from industry to industry; at the same time individual employers could always apply to the factory inspectors for permission to extend working hours, but this permission was not given unless the employer could show that he was unable to obtain additional labour.

Under the Weimar Republic, as was noted in Chapter 1, the eight-hour day was honoured more in the breach than in the observance, and the new Decree of July 1934 did not do more than continue the earlier tradition in this matter. In one respect it tightened up the regulations, for the former collective agreements allowed the employer to order overtime to be worked after consultation with the Works Council, whereas after the Decree overtime could only be worked if the authorisation of the factory inspector had been obtained, or by decision of the Trustees of Labour.

As the economic recovery proceeded and the shortage of labour became more acute the hours were lengthened. The general average of hours worked per day in all industries from January to September 1938 (7·69) was almost exactly the same as in 1929 (7·67), during the last boom. But in

1938 the average hours in the engineering industry were 8·34, and in the textile and clothing
industries only 7·26 and 7·30 respectively.

In April 1938 a new Hours of Work Decree
was issued to come into force on 1 January 1939.
The principal innovations introduced by the
Decree were:

(*a*) Hours of work might be spread over a
"triple week" of 144 hours instead of a fortnight,
as was provided by the earlier decrees.

(*b*) Taking over provisions which had already
been tried out experimentally by some Trustees
of Labour in their collective regulations, the Decree
introduced the making up, during a period of five
consecutive weeks, of hours of work lost owing
to local or public holidays, public displays, etc.

(*c*) The maximum number of hours that might
normally be worked on any one day, under the
spread-over rule, was fixed at ten, but extensions
beyond ten hours could be authorised by the
factory inspectors. Such extensions were facili-
tated by requiring that "urgent need" was a
sufficient ground, whereas authorisation could
previously be given "only in exceptional cases
for urgent reasons of public interest".

(*d*) The extent of payment for overtime was
reduced by the introduction of a rule that no extra
remuneration was due if the additional work

would have been permissible under the rules governing "work of preparation and extension".

(e) The Decree extended to all male adult workers a number of provisions which had hitherto been confined to salaried employees, women or young persons. The provisions in question related firstly to an unbroken period of rest of eleven hours in every twenty-four hours, and secondly to the grant of a break after not more than six hours' work. The duration of this was fixed at half an hour, but the single break might be replaced by two shorter breaks of a quarter of an hour each. These short breaks must be included in working hours.

An interesting Decree was also issued in December 1938 regulating weekly rest for hotel and restaurant staffs. These staffs were entitled to a continuous rest period of at least twenty-four hours immediately preceded or followed by a period of night rest. At least once a month the rest must fall on a Sunday. In watering places and holiday resorts the full day of rest might be replaced during the season by a half day. The factory inspectors were empowered, on sufficient grounds being given, to allow a different arrangement of rest periods.

In the first eight months of 1939, when the new Decree of April 1938 was in force, the ever-increasing shortage of skilled labour, and the intensification of the rearmament drive, led to a quite general adoption of the ten-hour working day over a large part of industry. In the iron and steel, coal-mining and building industries, it was not uncommon for twelve to fourteen hours to be worked daily, and the skilled men and foremen often worked still longer hours, as they had to be spread over shorter shifts of the less skilled workers. At the same time extensive advantage was taken of provisions for avoiding or diminishing payment for overtime, and in certain cases new collective regulations were issued by the Trustees of Labour which resulted in the lowering of existing wage rates. The economic pressure on men to work the maximum hours was thus enhanced. It was a very tired, over-strained working population, in all except the consumption-goods industries, which entered the war in September 1939.

When war broke out, practically all the protective provisions of the Hours of Work Decree were suspended; overtime pay for work in excess of eight hours and for Sunday and night work was abolished, and holidays with pay were also suspended. The employer had to continue to pay customary overtime rates, but instead of these going to the workers they were to be paid to the State.

It is clear from the available evidence that the response of the workers to these measures was to reduce so considerably their output that the Government were forced to withdraw the most stringent of the new provisions. From 15 November 1939 onwards the payment of overtime to the workers was once again permitted, but only after the tenth hour of work. The norm thus became the ten-hour day, but the factory inspectors were allowed in individual cases to permit longer hours, up to sixteen hours per day, by restricting the necessary rest periods to eight hours. The only limiting factor became "the health of the workers", which presumably was measured by the effects on their productivity. Holidays with pay were reinstated as from 15 January 1940.

It is possible that after the defeat of France, the authorities may have felt themselves able to shorten hours of work again, but the author has no information on this point.

WOMEN AND JUVENILES

In April 1938 a new Law, to come into force on 1 January 1939, was passed, regulating the labour of young persons, which was in many ways an advance on earlier legislation. The first part of the Law dealt with restrictions on the employment of children under fourteen years of age.[1] While

---

[1] The Law did not apply, however, to children in agriculture and domestic service, where child labour is by far the most common.

children were allowed to take part in household and family work and also in agriculture, their employment was prohibited in factories, work-shops or trade; but exemptions from the general rule could in special circumstances be made by the factory inspector, who was entitled to issue a "child labour licence" to children older than ten years of age. The daily working hours of children of school age, who received licences, were limited to four hours, and during school periods to two hours between 8 a.m. and 7 p.m.

The larger part of the new statute dealt with the working hours of young persons from fourteen to eighteen years of age (previously sixteen years). Any time spent in a vocational training school was to be included as part of working time, to be paid for by the employer. The normal working hours of women and young persons were fixed at eight hours daily and forty-eight hours weekly; but overtime, with a maximum of ten hours a day and of fifty hours a week, could be worked subject to permission from the factory inspector. All juveniles were to be entitled to one free afternoon a week, and to longer holidays with pay than those received by adults. The existing prohibition on the employment of women and young persons on Sundays and night work was maintained, and for the latter now covered those up to eighteen years of age.

Already, however, from the beginning of 1939 many of these protective measures were rendered inoperative by special Decrees issued at the end of 1938. Thus children from fourteen to sixteen were allowed, in spite of 'the new Law, to work until 10 o'clock at night in the iron and steel industries and the dockyards; and young workers sixteen to eighteen years of age were even allowed to do night work between 8 p.m. and 6 a.m. Women also were increasingly employed on night and Sunday work. With the outbreak of the war in September 1939 the protection of women and young persons was almost wholly withdrawn and overtime could be worked on the same scale as for adult males. The bad effects on health became so quickly apparent that by December 1939 it had been found necessary to reimpose a number of restrictions. Henceforward night work for women and young persons required the special permission of the Minister of Labour, while that of the factory inspectors had to be obtained for all work in excess of ten hours by women and young persons under eighteen. This meant that "regular" hours of work were eight per day, with a maximum of ten hours a day and fifty-six hours a week. Anything in excess of this was overtime, and both overtime and night work required special permission. For young persons from fourteen to sixteen, hours of work might not "as a rule" exceed fifty-four per week, this figure to include also time spent in a vocational training school.

PROTECTION AGAINST ACCIDENTS

Uniform regulations applying to the whole country were issued in April 1934 (previously each State had its own regulations), and in drafting them care was taken to have the co-operation and assistance of the factory inspectors. A considerable number of special orders were also issued applying to individual processes in which experience had shown that there was a liability to accident.

Nevertheless, with the expansion of output and employment, and especially the increase in hours and industrial fatigue, the absolute number of accidents increased appreciably after 1933, as can be seen from the following table:

	(1) Accidents giving rise to compensation payments	(2) Column (1) as percentage of insured persons in employment
1929	166,907	6·08
1932	67,650	3·62
1933	72,922	2·91
1934	80,951	3·06
1935	87,950	3·09
1936	86,792	2·89
1937	95,249	3·05

In the foregoing table column (2) is more sig-
nificant than column (1). The great decline (both
absolute and relative) from 1929 to 1932 was probably due to a considerable extent to changes in
the administration of the Accident Compensation
scheme, under the Emergency Decrees of 1931–32,
rather than to a genuine fall of this magnitude in
the number of the more serious type of accidents.
Since 1937 there has certainly been a considerable
increase in accidents, but later comparable figures
are not available.

HOME WORKERS

Home workers (*Heimarbeiter*) play an important,
if subsidiary, role in the German economy. There
are hundreds of thousands of them scattered over
the country, with occasional concentrations, as in
Thuringia and the Erzgebirge for toys, or in Upper
Franconia and the Vogtland district for clothing.
A census taken in 1937 showed that there were
over half a million home workers in Germany,
of whom 246,000 were engaged in the clothing
trades, 143,000 in spinning, 36,000 in the preparation of sweets, confectionery, etc., 23,000 in
woodwork and carving and 23,000 in making
musical instruments and toys. In addition there
were many other trades represented, such as

paper, glass, leather, brushes, jewellery, Christmas decorations, etc.

Home work may be broadly defined as certain forms of work carried out for an undertaking (often a middleman) outside its own premises, where the objects or materials made or worked up by the home workers are sold to the undertaking or handed over against payment for the work done. Though the home worker is legally independent of the undertaking for which he works, he is economically dependent on it; and the economic dependence is usually accompanied by a great inferiority of bargaining power and ignorance of conditions in the ultimate market.

There are three main types of domestic industry: in the first type it constitutes a whole time, all-the-year-round, occupation, as in some of the most highly skilled branches, where the standard of living may be fairly good; in the second it is merely a subsidiary occupation in the intervals of other work which is the main livelihood, as in the case of peasants in the winter months; in the third, and most widely extended, it is an essential means of eking out an existence which otherwise would be on an intolerably low level, as in many of the isolated mountain valleys, where the soil will only grow potatoes and is too poor to carry much live stock. It is this last type in which the poverty

and misery have been greatest and which most
stood in need of assistance.

No action was taken towards the protection of
home workers until 1911, when a House Work
Law was passed requiring the keeping of a register
of home workers, the posting up of price lists for
work done, and the fulfilment of certain health
conditions in domestic workshops. It appears,
however, to have accomplished very little in practice. Then in 1923 an amended Home Work Law
was passed which empowered technical committees to fix binding rates of pay, and to impose
fines when the minimum rates were not paid. But
the procedure was a complicated one, supervision
was inadequate, and the conditions of large
sections of the home workers still remained
deplorable.

A more comprehensive regulation of the whole
problem was attempted by the Home Work Law
of March 1934. Under this Law twenty-three
special Trustees of Labour were appointed for
individual branches of home work, with power
to issue collective regulations (*Tarifordnungen*)
governing the remuneration of home workers,
and some 600 of these regulations had been issued
by 1938. The preparation of these lists was a highly
complex problem owing to the immense variety
of conditions prevailing, but the general principle

adopted was to fix price rates so as to afford an adequate remuneration on the basis of a reasonable number of working hours. The interpretation of "adequate remuneration" varies widely according to whether the work in question constitutes merely a minor and subsidiary form of earnings, or whether it is the sole and main source of livelihood of the home worker. Rate fixing had also always to take into account the extent to which the market could carry higher labour costs, and this again varied greatly. There were certain products enjoying almost a monopoly position, such as Christmas-tree decorations, and some branches of basket making; but particularly in these, owing to the isolation of the home workers, remuneration had been depressed to a very low level, with the result that their quality had also deteriorated. In these cases relatively high rates were fixed on the basis of good quality production, and were rigidly enforced even at the cost of driving some of the inferior grades off the market altogether.

Further, although it was not universally possible, the collective regulations contained provisions that whenever these could be arranged home workers should also enjoy the benefits of holidays with pay, and this was carried out in all the more important branches. In December 1937 the Decree, providing for the full payment of wages on public holidays to all industrial workers, was extended so far as circumstances would permit to home workers.

Finally, it may be mentioned that, largely through the efforts of the Labour Front, direct steps were taken to increase the demand for the products of some of the poorest classes of home workers. Thus, the millions of badges which are constantly being sold throughout Germany in the streets (118,700,000 badges were sold in 1936–37), especially in connection with the *Winterhilfe* collections, are made for the most part by these home workers and not in factories.

It is not without interest to note that, in spite of the preoccupations of the war, time was found to issue on 30 October 1939 a Decree amending the Home Work Law of 23 March 1934. This Decree extended the scope of protection for home workers to other categories of persons not previously covered, and tightened up the provisions for securing that the officially established remuneration is in fact paid to all home workers. It also increased the penalties, and simplified their collection, in the event of non-fulfilment of the conditions laid down in the collective regulations issued by the Trustees of Labour.

The German Minister of Labour at the end of 1938 declared proudly that the general conditions of the home workers and their protection from exploitation were better in Germany than in any other country and that many foreign experts had come to Germany to study the methods of regulations employed there. So far as Great Britain is concerned it may be pointed out, on the one hand, that home work has nothing like the importance in this country that it has in Germany; and on the other, that the Trade Board system (in which the trade unions play a vital part) has proved for many years past an effective method of protecting and raising the standard of living of the home worker here.[1]

[1] A home worker as defined by the Trade Boards is a person who works in his or her own home, or in any place not under the control or management of the employer. "Of the forty-seven industries having Trade Boards in 1937, home work exists to some degree in nearly half." D. Sells, *British Wages Boards. A Study in Industrial Democracy*, p. 197.

CHAPTER V

SOCIAL INSURANCE

As a result of the great inflation which culminated in 1923, the system of social insurance, which had been built up in the twenty years preceding the war of 1914–18, suffered severe damage. In particular the actuarial basis of the whole Pensions Insurance (old age, invalidity, widows and orphans) was destroyed owing to the wiping out of the reserves. In this latter and, in many ways, most important branch of social insurance, it had been found necessary to abandon the normal principle of collective accumulation with a general average contribution, or, as it is sometimes called, "reversion covering",[1] and to adopt the "assessment method" by which only current outgoings are covered by the contributors. In the boom of 1927–29 it would have been possible to return to a sounder basis, but instead of doing this the Government, very understandably, decided to introduce an unemployment insurance scheme

---

[1] Under the "reversion covering" method the contributions are so calculated that they cover not only the claims of the present recipients of pensions, but also the prospective claims of all existing and future members.

involving heavy contributions from both employers and insured persons. The depression of
1930–32, besides crippling the finances of the
unemployment insurance scheme, reacted very
badly on the pensions schemes, since it led, as
might be expected, to a large increase in the number of claims for pensions.

The task of consolidating the financial structure
of the system of social insurance, with which the
National Socialist Government was faced, was
made very much easier by the great decline in
unemployment from 1933 onwards, which raised
the ratio of active contributors to recipients of
pensions. The first important step was taken by
the Law of 7 December 1933, under which the
Pensions Insurance received an increased permanent subsidy from the Reich; the methods of
calculating future pensions were revised so as to
diminish their amount; pensions which had been
improperly awarded were withdrawn, and contribution and benefit categories were revised;
finally it was provided that at some future date,
when unemployment had decreased sufficiently,
part of the contributions to Unemployment Insurance should be transferred to the Pensions
Insurance. As a result of this measure, the National
Socialists were able to announce the re-adoption
of the "reversion covering" method so far as

Pensions Insurance was concerned. It was not, however, until an amending Law was passed in December 1937 that the contemplated transfer actually took place, and then only in a partial form. Under this Law annual sums representing 18 % and 25 % respectively of the contribution income of the Wage Earners and Salaried Employees' Pensions Insurance were transferred to it from Unemployment Insurance. Even this did not completely solve the problem, and by the same Law the Reich took over the ultimate financial responsibility for the whole of the capital liabilities of the Pensions Funds. The Law of December 1937 also provided for an annual transfer from the general Pensions Funds to the specially hard-hit Miners' Pension Funds (*Knapp-schaftsversicherung*).

The finances of the sickness and accident insurance schemes had been much less seriously affected by the events subsequent to 1918, and no drastic action was necessary here to make them naturally sound.

In the case of Unemployment Insurance, subsidies from the Reich were still necessary in 1933. From 1934 onwards the continuous decline in unemployment, accompanied as it was by unaltered rates of contributions, led to ever-increasing surpluses. Prior to 1938 these were simply transferred to the Reich for its general purposes (chiefly rearmament). But since the end of 1937 the surpluses have been used for subsidising the branches of social insurance, for financing marriage loans and family allowances, and for "accumulating a reserve against the possibility of future unemployment". Soon after the war broke out, by a Decree of 5 September 1939, the character of the Unemployment Insurance Scheme was radically altered. All conditions as to the number of contributions, employment in insured trades, etc., were abolished, and in their place was substituted a simple provision that "every one is entitled to relief if he is available for work but is involuntarily unemployed". All relief is subject to a means test and may be made conditional on the applicant undergoing a course of re-training, or carrying out any work for the benefit of the community that may be assigned to him. The high level of the contributions to Unemployment Insurance has, however, been maintained unaltered.

As in the case of Great Britain, so too in Germany, social insurance had assumed many different local forms in the course of its development. Some of the insurance bodies were small and weak and there was no co-ordination between them. By a general Law of 5 July 1934, the different types of sickness funds (local funds, rural funds, works funds and guild funds) were to remain for the time being unchanged, but an equalisation fund was to be set up to be administered by the Pensions Insurance authorities for all the sickness funds in their areas. The Pensions Insurance authorities were also entrusted with the administration both of the hospitals, sanatoria, convalescent homes, etc., which had been established by the sickness funds, and of the general services provided for the prevention of disease. At the same time, the system of self-government, which had previously existed throughout social insurance, was replaced by authoritarian rule in accordance with the leadership principle. Every insurance institution was placed under the control of a leader, who as a rule was a permanent public official; with him was associated an advisory board composed of insured persons and employers in equal numbers, together with a doctor and a representative of the local authority.

Further steps towards the unification of social insurance were taken in 1937 by the compulsory federation of the various types of funds in each of the main groups of insurance, and by conferring on these federations the status of public bodies, as also by the financial readjustments referred to above. Apart from federation, many of the smaller societies were merged in larger ones; thus the number of separate sickness funds, which in 1933 was 6387, had fallen by 1938 to 4565. In September 1939 the last vestiges of self-government in social insurance were abolished and even the advisory boards were swept away.

As the financial position of the insurance schemes improved, it was found possible to extend the scope of insurance to cover additional sections of the population, and also to restore some of the cuts in benefits which had been made by emergency decrees in 1932. In December 1937 the right was given to all German citizens, whether at home or abroad, who were below the age of forty years, to join the voluntary Pensions Insurance. A year later the whole group of four and a half million handicraftsmen (*Handwerker*) was brought within the scope of the compulsory Pensions Insurance. Account was taken, however, of the fact that many handicraftsmen had already taken out private life insurance policies, and these were exempted from the payment of contributions so long as their existing payments were not less than those for which they would have been liable under the Salaried Employees' Pension Insurance. Alternatively, a handicraftsman could either be fully insured under the Pensions Scheme or pay half his contributions to the Pensions Fund and half to a private insurance company. Other minor changes of scope were the inclusion of independent teachers and theatrical artistes in Sickness Insurance, of both theatrical artistes and journalists in Pensions Insurance, and of members of the Labour Service and of those taking part in training schemes, in Accident Insurance.

At the same time the benefits in various directions were improved, most considerably perhaps in the case of the Pensions Funds, by the encouragement of additional voluntary insurance within the scope of the scheme by agreement between the worker and employer. Such additional payments were strongly encouraged by the Labour Front and were counted amongst the qualifying conditions in the annual competitions for the designation of a "model business". The table on p. 91 shows for a salaried employee, with an assumed income of 500–600 marks per month (paying a normal monthly contribution of 12.50 marks with an additional payment of 10 marks monthly, the employer contributing 12.50 marks *plus* 15 marks), the effect of such additional insurance.

It may be noted further that in the event of a worker or salaried employee falling upon evil days (during a period of unemployment his contributions to sickness and pensions are in any case paid by the Unemployment Insurance Fund) he can keep his reversionary rights in the Pensions

Insurance alive so long as he can pay or has paid half the contributions in respect of his total insurance period.

Age in years	Period of insurance in years	Pension received in event of invalidity or old age			Pensions as percentage of income of 6600 marks annually
		From basic insurance annually Marks	From additional insurance annually Marks	Total insurance annually Marks	
36	6	576	360	936	14
40	10	720	600	1320	20
50	20	1080	1200	2280	35
60	30	1440	1800	3240	49
65	35	1620	2100	3720	56

The German social insurance system has always prided itself on its care for the preventive side of medical treatment, and the National Socialists claim that they have fully maintained and extended this preventive and remedial work. But the extent to which the population has been overdriven in recent years and the tremendous pressure under which large sections of it have been living, must have counteracted a good deal of the value of this work. There are unfortunately no detailed statistics available for a later year than 1937, but it is officially stated that in the fifty-six large cities, comprising about one-third of the German

population, the death-rate, which was 10·3 per
thousand in 1932, rose to 11·4 in 1938 and 12·1
in 1939. The rise in 1939 was ascribed to an
influenza epidemic and long-continued cold in
the first half of that year. Even if this were
the whole explanation, it may point to a lowered
vitality such as might well arise from over-
exertion combined with a shortage in certain
important constituents in diet. Nevertheless this
is only presumptive evidence, and it would not
be safe to deduce too much from these figures;
for example the rate for 1939 was still below that
for London in 1937 (12·5 per 1000) and considerably lower than that for Liverpool (13·7) or
Glasgow (14·6). Variations of the order of 1 or 2
per 1000 have also frequently occurred in the past
in both Britain and Germany in successive years.[1]

Finally, something may be said as to certain
general economic features of social insurance. It
is well known that ever since 1937 Germany has
been forcing rearmament and other forms of public
investment so hard that, on the one hand she has
had to fight hard against the inflationary effects
of the rise of money incomes, not accompanied

[1] See an article in the *Nineteenth Century*, September 1940,
by Dr W. A. Brend: "Public Health in Germany", for a
very damaging analysis of the highly coloured and misleading
statistics published by Dr M. Gumpert in his book *Heil
Hunger*.

by a parallel growth in the output of consumption goods; and on the other hand she has had difficulty in financing the immense volume of capital expenditure. Now every extension of the scope of social insurance has both helped to contract the size of money incomes and also, in so far as there has been a surplus of revenue over expenditure, has provided additional funds for the Government. Thus in the two years 1937 and 1938 the social insurance funds (excluding Unemployment Insurance) increased their reserves by 2000 million marks. In June 1938 the capital assets of the Pensions Funds amounted to over 6000 million marks, of which one-third was held in the form of loans issued by the Reich.

The widening of the scope of social insurance is clearly a good thing in itself, while the accumulation of reserves in the Pensions Funds can be abundantly justified by the earlier financial history of these funds, and by the need for making provision for future claims which must increase with the rise in the average age of the German population due to the decline in the birth-rate after the war of 1914–18. At the same time it is clear that the attractiveness of this type of social reform was enhanced in the eyes of the Government by the fact that it would also subserve the wider political and economic policies of the régime.

CHAPTER VI

SOCIAL ASSISTANCE; POPULATION POLICY

SOCIAL ASSISTANCE

So far as general public assistance is concerned the National Socialists have maintained the provisions of the Public Assistance Orders passed in 1924 by the Weimar Republic. Under these Orders Public Assistance is administered through State and District Public Assistance Unions (*Fürsorgeverbände*). A person who cannot provide a sufficient subsistence for himself and his dependents through his own labour or means, and who is not given such subsistence by other persons, in particular by his relations, is deemed to be in need. A sufficient assistance comprises:

(*a*) Maintenance proper, including housing, food and clothing, etc.

(*b*) Medical aid in case of sickness and the aid required for the recovery of working capacity.

(*c*) Maternity aid.

(*d*) General and vocational education for young persons.

(*e*) Vocational education for the blind, deaf and dumb, and cripples.

The National Socialist régime has, however, extended the existing welfare provisions in a number of directions. The disabled soldiers who had been wounded in the war 1914–18 were the object of special care, and an Act was passed requiring all firms to reserve a certain proportion of places for severely injured persons, which included both ex-soldiers and those who had been the victims of industrial accidents. As the general shortage of labour grew more acute it became possible to absorb these men increasingly into industry, with the result that the number of disabled war veterans who were unemployed fell from 47,000 in March 1933 to 9500 in March 1938. Supplementary grants were also made to disabled ex-service men and to the dependents of those who had fallen in the war. Similar grants were made from public funds to the small pensioners whose pension rights had been virtually extinguished owing to the inflation of 1921–23, and to those old age and invalidity pensioners who were unable to live on their pensions.

The new régime has in addition set up its own Party organisation for supplementing the ordinary State channels for the distribution of relief. This consists of the National Socialist Welfare Organisation (*Nationalsozialistische Volkswohlfahrt*), generally known by the letters N.S.V. It has over seven million members and seeks both to awaken and to canalise, in an organised and conscious form, the charitable impulses of the mass of the people towards their less fortunate fellow-country-men.

The largest and most spectacular of these activities of the N.S.V. is the Winter Relief (*Winterhilfe*). Every winter an army of collectors appears on the streets selling badges; apart from this, on one Sunday in the month there is an obligatory one-course midday meal throughout Germany, the saving resulting from which has to be contributed to the Winter Relief Fund; further, every worker in employment pays a graded sum from his weekly or monthly earnings towards the Winter Relief, ranging from a few Pfennigs weekly in the case of the ordinary wage-earner to larger, but still relatively small, sums for employees with higher incomes, e.g. a salaried employee with 400 marks a month would pay 2.5 marks a month = 60 Pfennigs a week, to Winter Relief. Finally levies of a quasi-compulsory character in cash or in kind are made from peasants, farmers, employers and the middle classes generally. These levies are fixed arbitrarily by the collecting members of the National Socialist Party and can amount to a veritable imposition.

The sums involved are very large, as can be

seen from the following table showing the value
of the assistance given by the Winter Relief from
1933 to 1937:

	Marks
1933–34	350,000,000
1934–35	360,500,000
1935–36	371,900,000
1936–37	408,300,000

Practically the whole of the relief given by this
organisation is made in kind, and consists prin-
cipally in food, coal and clothing; it is all given
during the winter months. In 1936–37 the chief
items distributed were potatoes, 11 million cwt.;
domestic fuel, 42·5 million cwt.; sundry foodstuffs, 2·5 million cwt.; clothing, shoes, household
linen, beds, bedding, etc., 13·6 million pieces or
pairs; free meals, school and Winter Relief meals,
33 million.

To collect or distribute this vast amount of
money and goods an army of voluntary helpers has
been forthcoming to the number of 1,350,000, and
it is contended by the National Socialists that the
expenses of administration, which are put at 1·8 %
of the relief given in 1936–37, are kept very low
for this reason.

But who are the recipients of this colossal
charity? It was originally laid down that the
beneficiaries should be "unemployed persons,
workers on short time, war victims, war widows,

pensioners under social insurance schemes, persons in receipt of poor relief and other necessitous persons". The list is a comprehensive one and was certainly broadly interpreted, for in the winter of 1933–34 as many as 253 out of every 1000 inhabitants (one-quarter of the whole population) received help from Winter Relief. As a result of the decline in unemployment this figure had fallen considerably by 1936–37, but was still 161 persons in every thousand of the population.[1] In the years 1933–34 the average value of the goods received per head (men, women, and children) amounted to 21 marks, and in 1936–37 to 37 marks.

It is not easy to assess the positive value of Winter Relief. Like everything else of this order which is done by the Nazis it is organised on a vast scale and is given the maximum publicity and propaganda so as to enhance its popular appeal. Two things must be remembered: firstly, Winter Relief is in addition to the other forms of poor relief and to the charitable efforts of the Churches, and a good deal goes to those who for various reasons would not be eligible for ordinary State relief; secondly, there are and always have been in Germany large numbers of persons

[1] In 1937–38 the figure was 130 persons in every thousand of the population.

existing on a cash income so small that it would appear incredible to the average Englishman that they could live at all; even a little extra help can mean a good deal in these circumstances. Moreover, the German winter is long and hard; there is normally a good deal of protracted seasonal unemployment, and even in our own country the Unemployment Assistance Board has recently recognised the need for supplementing the normal allowances by additional grants during the winter months.

Thus, although goods to the value of 30 to 40 marks, spread over a period of from four to five months, may not sound much, they may yet make an appreciable difference if the family budget is as small as is often the case in Germany.

It is, of course, true that if the poor could reason like an economist, they might turn round on their rulers and say: "What you give us in Winter Relief and the like is a very inadequate return for what you take from us by your policy of heavy taxation, self-sufficiency, high food prices and frenzied rearmament, and now finally war." But the propaganda machine, the censorship, and the Secret Police, are there to see that such thoughts do not become vocal, and unless they are widely published it is probable that they will not formulate themselves clearly in the minds of many.

High policy is too difficult for the ordinary man; much poverty exists under every social system, and unless they are driven to desperation the masses will submit to whatever system of government is imposed upon them.

Another main institution set up by the N.S.V. is known as Mother and Child (*Mutter und Kind*), and is also on a very large scale. The chief purpose of this is to provide a nation-wide service of advice, instruction and help for young mothers and for children, especially those below school age. Recuperation homes are made available for mothers after child-birth, nurseries and kindergartens have been provided, in particular in the country districts, for looking after the young children during harvest time when the mothers are in the fields, and a network of advisory health centres has been established all over Germany. In general the aim is to diminish infant and child mortality, to raise the standard of health in the early years of child life, and to emphasise the importance of preventive and remedial measures as a means of diminishing poverty.

Winter Relief and Mother and Child are the two chief activities of the N.S.V., but in its task of relieving distress it operates also in many other directions, which reasons of space make it impossible to enumerate.

One final observation may be permitted which bears upon the whole of this aspect of German social policy. The millions of voluntary workers carrying on the work of administration for the N.S.V., and many others besides, have been in a large measure successfully imbued with the ideals which it has professed: a sense of social responsibility, a feeling for the interdependence of all sections of the people, and a readiness to make sacrifices on behalf of what is held to be the common good.

POPULATION POLICY

In Germany as in other Western countries the birth-rate had been falling faster than the death-rate for many years. The net reproduction rate,[1] which was 1·448 in 1881–90, was only 0·924 in 1924–26. But the great depression of 1930–32 led to a further violent fall in the rate to 0·748 in 1931 and to 0·698 in 1932.

The National Socialists initiated a tremendous drive against what they regarded as a threatened

[1] The net reproduction rate represents the number of girl babies who will be born to the survivors of every thousand girls born in the previous generation, on the basis of the fertility and mortality rates prevailing at any one time. A rate of 1·0 means that each newly born girl will just replace herself, so that a continuance of this rate would mean that the population would ultimately become stationary.

race suicide. They introduced stronger penalties against illegal abortion, which had been extensively practised in the years since the last war. But their main positive measures consisted in marriage loans and subsidies, increased tax-abatements for dependents, family allowances, and propaganda, together with the general revival of employment and business activity.[1]

The original intention of the Law for the provision of marriage loans, which came into force in August 1933, appears to have been to withdraw women from the labour market and to stimulate the market for consumption-goods. The loans take the form of coupons exchangeable for household goods, varying in value from 300 to 1000 marks; there is no income limit, but those who want the loans must show that they could not otherwise afford to furnish a home. They bear no interest and have to be repaid at 1% monthly, so that the loan would be refunded in just over eight years. The birth of a child during the repayment period cancels one-fourth of the original loan, and for families of four children the whole loan becomes a gift. From August

[1] A constituent element in Nazi population policy, and one which in the present state of biological knowledge would seem to be open to grave objection, is the practice of compulsory sterilisation under a Law for the Prevention of Hereditarily Diseased Offspring, which was passed in 1934.

1933 to the end of 1938 a total of 1,121,000 loans was granted, with an average value of about 660 marks per loan; and in 980,365 cases parts of the loans were cancelled as a result of the birth of a child, though it would obviously be unsafe to assume that this was a case of *post hoc ergo propter hoc*.[1]

Apart from satisfying sundry requirements, such as racial stock, political views, freedom from inheritable defects, etc., the original condition for the receipt of a marriage loan was that the wife should give up her employment and should not re-enter the employment market unless her husband became in need of help. But this proviso began to be relaxed towards the end of 1936 and was completely abolished after 1 November 1937.

The loans were financed at first by a special tax on unmarried men and women, but they were later merged into the general structure of income tax, which provides heavy abatements for children. From December 1937 onwards a part of the surplus of the Unemployment Insurance Fund was allocated to the finance of marriage loans.

[1] It may be noted that by 31 December 1933, only five months after the first granting of loans to newly married couples, 13,610 loans were partly cancelled as a result of the birth of a child, and the number had risen by 31 March 1934, eight months after these loans were established, to 43,108, representing a partial cancellation of more than a fifth of the total number of loans granted to that date.

In addition to marriage loans and tax abatements, grants were given to families with dependent children. In September 1935, single lump sum donations were made, up to 100 marks, for each child under the age of sixteen, with a maximum of 160 marks for a given family. These grants were given on investigation of the family circumstances, and if it appeared that the parents could not by their own efforts provide the goods necessary for the household. They were also confined to families with numerous children, normally six or more. Since July 1936, family allowances have been granted on a monthly basis (*laufende Kinderbeihilfen*) and their scope has been greatly extended by a decree of March 1938. The upper income limit is now 8000 marks per annum; the allowances are available for each child up to twenty-one years of age, provided they are still dependent; the grants amount to 10 marks per month each for the third and fourth children and 20 marks per month for the fifth and each additional child;[1] finally, the Ministry of Finance is now empowered to give educational assistance for enabling the children of families with four or

[1] A worker with ten children, earning 160 marks per month, receives 140 marks per month in family allowances, not subject to any deduction. As nearly 20% of his earnings are deducted for various contributions, his family allowance in effect would amount to more than his ordinary working income.

more living children to attend secondary or technical schools—these grants may include, in addition to school fees, a payment of 600 marks per annum to cover the cost incurred for children who have to study away from their homes.

There is a still more favourable type of marriage loan available for agricultural workers, and other measures include reductions in railway fares, and the construction of specially cheap houses for those with large families.

The table on the following page sets out the most important population statistics.

It will be seen that there has been a very remarkable increase in births since 1933. "In 1938 fertility still appeared to be rising and was probably very close to full replacement level in that year."[1] The really essential question is how far this increase can be attributed to the measures adopted by the National Socialist régime.

Now it must be borne in mind that the years 1931–33 were a period of extremely heavy unemployment and great depression of trade. The birth-rate in those years was abnormally low, and was bound in any case to recover to a considerable extent as soon as there was a revival of economic activity and a decrease of unemployment. Many

---

[1] D. V. Glass, *Population Policies and Movements in Europe*, p. 305.

GERMANY (*including the* SAAR)

Year	No. of marriages	Live births	Crude birth-rate per 1000 of population	Deaths	Excess of births over deaths (net increase of population)	Rate per 1000 of population	Total population (thousands)
1913	513,283	1,838,750	27·5	1,004,950	833,800	12·4	66,978
1928	594,631	1,199,998	18·6	747,444	452,554	7·0	64,393
1932	516,793	993,126	15·1	707,642	285,484	4·3	65,716
1933	638,573	971,174	14·7	737,877	233,297	3·5	66,032 ‡
1934	740,165	1,198,350	18·0	724,758	473,592	7·1	66,409
1935	651,435	1,263,976	18·9	792,018	471,958	7·1	66,871
1936	609,631	1,277,952	19·0	795,203	481,849	7·2	67,346
1937	620,265	1,277,046	18·8	794,367	492,679	7·1	67,900
1938	644,363	1,346,911	19·7	800,571	546,340	8·0	—
1939	760,000*†	1,420,000*	20·5*	—	—	—	69,316‡

* Estimated. (*Wirtschaft und Statistik*. Feb. 1940, pp. 66–7.)

† The big jump in marriages was mainly due to war marriages in the latter part of 1939.

‡ Census figures.

marriages had been postponed until better times made them possible. But when full account is taken of these and other "natural" causes, it seems certain that the continuous increase in the German birth-rate down to 1938 must in part be attributed to State intervention.

Mr D. V. Glass, to whose admirable book[1] this section is largely indebted, and who is a high authority on the subject, attaches the greatest weight to the highly effective discouragement of abortion. He places second in the scale of importance the economic and financial measures, such as marriage loans, family allowances and tax rebates, while he rates quite low the factor which tends to assume the chief place in the eyes of German writers on the subject—the change of attitude, what they term the "Psychic re-birth" of the people, due to the force of the ideas and achievements of National Socialism. While in agreement with Mr Glass as to the relative importance of the first two of the above factors, the present writer would be inclined to give greater weight than Mr Glass does to the psychological factor, *for the period down to the end of* 1938. That its effects would have been continuous and permanent seems most unlikely, but that there was some direct, appreciable connection between

[1] Cited above on p. 105 *n.*

the rise in the birth-rate and the atmosphere of
hope and creative activity which characterised
Germany between 1933 and 1938, does appear
probable.[1] The very effectiveness of the legal
measures adopted to check abortion is probably
to be explained in part on psychological grounds.
The war, of course, upsets all estimates and fore-
casts of what will be the future trend of the
German population.

Finally, there remains for consideration the
significance of this population policy in its relation
to social welfare in general and to the attitude of
the mass of the people to the National Socialist
State. On the one hand it would not be plausible
to suggest that the financial and other measures
of help extended to those with families had actually
made parenthood profitable; hence to the extent
to which people have been induced to marry and
have children or enlarge their families, they are
presumably worse off *financially* than they would

[1] In the light of subsequent events this statement may strike
many readers as an unduly favourable view of Nazi Germany,
even for the period to which it relates. The author can only
record his conviction, based partly on personal observation in
Germany in 1938, that at that time the great bulk of the
German people (as distinct from the inner ring of leaders)
were thinking of anything rather than war, and were inspired
by the economic and social changes which they felt were
taking place around them and which seemed to hold out such
high hopes for the future. Their eyes were turned inwards
and not outwards.

otherwise have been. On the other hand the marriage loans represent quite a substantial dowry to the marriageable girl; moreover, many marriages would in any event have taken place and children been born even without the loans and the family allowances, and in all these cases they constitute a net advantage to be set on the credit side of the régime. The benefits are felt particularly by the women, and it is amongst their ranks that many of the staunchest supporters of Hitler are to be found. The population policy of the National Socialists must be reckoned as one of the most apparently successful, as well as one of the most generally popular of their achievements.

Chapter VII

HOUSING POLICY

When the National Socialists came into power they announced the coming of a new era of house building which would make good the faults and shortcomings of the past. They accused the housing policy of their predecessors of neglecting the needs of the workers for dwellings at low rents; of concentrating on the construction of vast tenement blocks in the large cities; and in general of a lack of planning and order.

Here, as in many other (though not all) aspects of social policy, the promises of the National Socialists outran their performance. Field-Marshal Göring's phrase "Guns instead of Butter" would have been even more appropriately worded "Guns instead of Houses"; for nowhere were the competing claims of rearmament more decisive than in this sphere. High policy here cut across the lines of an activity which the new régime itself recognised as being of very great importance.

Great emphasis was laid in the first place on the need for decentralisation of the population as far as possible. Partly, no doubt, this had strategic ends in view especially after the promulgation

of the Second Four Year Plan in 1936, since the
new raw material factories were deliberately constructed in the interior of Germany away from
the existing centres of population. But it also
conformed to a general desire to create smaller
towns in which the contact between the urban
dweller and the country round him was still maintained. In actual fact the great cities have continued to grow, but large housing estates have been
developed on the outskirts, and these have been
combined, wherever possible, with allotments.
At the same time many new towns have arisen
in connection with the raw material factories,
such as the Hermann Göring Works at Salz-
gitter in Brunswick or the People's Car Works at
Fallersleben.

Secondly, building has been planned throughout both as to materials and style and also location.
All over Germany regional and town planning
has been developed to a high degree along very
efficient lines. There is a Central Planning Board
in Berlin; a Reichs Institute, linked up with all
the Universities, for conducting research into
problems of planning; and regional planning
authorities in every State of the Reich. The latter
must be consulted before a road can be constructed,
a factory built or a housing scheme approved,
while the Central Board is concerned with laying

down general lines of policy for the whole country. An immense activity is going on in this field; it represents one of the less known but most constructive aspects of modern Germany, and is one that may well provide valuable lessons for other countries.

Thirdly, the desire of the National Socialists has been to encourage the building of small houses to hold from one to four families, in place of the many-storied blocks of flats. Here again the relative expensiveness of this type of construction, and the urgent need of the large cities, have meant that a large amount of new construction has continued to consist of flats. Still, a great number of working-class houses have been built even in the cities, and this represents a new type of working-class housing in Germany. Between 1933 and 1937, 63·2 % of the new dwellings constructed were in the form of houses and only 36·8 % were in blocks of flats.

Fourthly, it is sought to establish small housing settlements and homesteads, in which the occupier will be able to supplement his industrial earnings by the produce he can derive from his land. These settlements are the peculiar pride of the National Socialists, and are for them the kernel of their housing policy. Towards the end of the Weimar Republic a start had been made at providing settlements, especially on the outskirts of towns, as a part of unemployment policy; but it has been much developed, from a more general standpoint, by the National Socialists. Between 1933 and 1938 some 457 million marks had been supplied from Reich sources for the furtherance of small settlements, and financial aid had been given from public funds for the construction of 155,000 homesteads. As, however, not everybody is fitted for this type of settlement, public funds have also been provided on a considerable scale for the so-called *Volkswohnungen* or people's houses. These are small houses built cheaply with the aid of loans at specially low rates of interest, and let at low rents to those who cannot afford the more expensive type of accommodation. Lastly, the flight from the land has led the National Socialists to devote special attention to agricultural housing where the shortage has been very great, though not so obvious as in the large cities. Down to October 1938 the building of some 35,000 houses for agricultural workers had been subsidised by the Reich, of which nearly one-third dated from March 1937 when additional measures were taken to accelerate this type of construction.

During the Weimar Republic, owing partly to the cost of building and partly to the high rates of interest, housing had been largely financed by public funds, chiefly from the house-rent tax; foreign capital also was used to some extent for building purposes.

Under the new régime the mortgage rate was lowered from 8–10 % to $4\frac{1}{3}$ %, and so far as possible housing was financed from individual savings, public funds being only used to subsidise building in cases where private savings were insufficient, or in order to reduce rents for the low-income classes. The normal method of financing a building is that about half the cost of the house is borrowed from a mortgage bank, insurance company or savings bank on a first mortgage at a rate between 4 and 5 %. A further 25 % of the value of the land and building can be obtained on a second mortgage, which involves a higher rate of interest owing to the greater risk. Here the Reich has stepped in with a guarantee in cases where the building is of the type that it wishes to encourage. It is estimated that one-third of all the dwellings constructed in Germany in recent years have been provided with a Reich guarantee for the second mortgage. The remaining 25 % in ordinary circumstances will be met by the house owner, but in the case of small settlements and working-class houses the Reich gives subsidies up to a maximum amount of 90 % of the total value. The balance of 10 or 15 % is left for the house owner or his family to find, but employers are encouraged to make grants or loans to their employees to close this final gap, and it is estimated that in 1937, 11·4 % of the total extra finance required for small dwellings, in addition to the first and second mortgages, was supplied by employers.

Taking the total gross figures of construction since the last war, it will be found that 2,837,000 dwellings (including conversions) were constructed in the fourteen years 1919–32, or an average of 200,000 per annum; while the corresponding figure for the six years 1933–38 was 1,800,000, or an average of 300,000 per annum.

From what has been said it is evident that the National Socialists have taken seriously the housing shortage which dates from the last war, and that they have made considerable efforts to deal with it. Yet all that they have accomplished in this direction has been far below what has been needed, and far below what could have been achieved had it not been for the competing claims of rearmament. When they came into office there was an estimated shortage of one million dwellings; yet in spite of the construction of 1,800,000 dwellings between 1933 and the end of 1938, the estimated shortage at the latter date was as high as one and a half million dwellings. The increase in the number of marriages, and the very success of their population policy, increased the need for housing, with the result that they did not even contrive to keep pace with the growth of the demand.

Nevertheless, when the matter is looked at from the point of view of the German people themselves, their Government can claim and take credit for very substantial achievements in house building, the evidence of which is everywhere to be seen. In one year, 1937, more dwellings were built than in any other single year since the war of 1914–18, and the fact that still more might have been done is probably less evident to the majority of German people than it is to the outside observer of the National Socialist régime.

Chapter VIII

CONCLUSIONS

THE short passage placed at the back of the title-page of this book is taken from *Searchlight on Europe* by Mr John de Courcy. This book consists largely of reprints of the generally well-informed monthly *Memoranda of Information* circulated by the so-called Imperial Policy Group, of which Mr Kenneth de Courcy is the editor. Prior to the war the Group had observers travelling about Germany and other parts of Europe and most of the data was derived from reports of these observers. The statement here reproduced corresponds with the present writer's impressions of the state of affairs in Germany during the first half of 1938. That it should still be possible to employ such terms when considering the attitude of the German workers, as late as April 1939, is rather remarkable as by then the drive for greater output had led to a great increase in hours of work in the munitions and constructional industries, and the drastic decrees of 1939 for mobilising labour were already in force. Whether "contentment" or "apathy" would be the better term with which to describe the state of mind of a considerable section, especially of the older members of the working classes in Germany, is perhaps arguable; but even a blend of the two is something far removed from that impression of a whole population groaning under mass oppression and exploitation, which most propaganda writers in this country seek to convey as typical of present-day Germany.

In writing this little book the present writer has had two main objects in view: first, to give as comprehensive and impartial a description as possible of what has been done in National Socialist Germany in the way of social policy, and secondly, to explain how it is possible that such a statement as that quoted from Mr de Courcy could be true. If the statement was even broadly true, then such a picture as that presented in, for example, Dr W. A. Robson's *Labour Policy in Nazi Germany*,[1] cannot also be true, or at least cannot be the whole truth.

That there is discontent among sections of the German working classes, owing, above all, to the lengthening of the hours of work even since 1937, is of course undeniable. No one could read the monthly reports of the Executive Committee of the Social Democratic Party, published in Paris,

[1] Oxford University Pamphlets, 1940.

without realising, if he had not realised it before, that beneath the apparently orderly regimented surface of German social life there are latent forces of opposition which may one day acquire a truly formidable cohesion and strength, in which they are at present totally lacking. But two things must be borne in mind: in the first place, the average German is an inveterate grumbler and will remain so under any type of régime as far as he dares, hence it is easy to exaggerate the significance of such individual grumbling; secondly, it would be no more legitimate to accept at their face value, as giving a valid *general* description of working-class opinion in Germany, the reports of the Executive Committee just referred to than it would have been to accept the reports on the state of opinion in Russia, derived from under-ground channels by White Russians living in Paris during the first ten years of the Bolshevik Revolution. On the one hand we cannot ignore evidence of this character, but on the other it would be very unwise to attach too great a significance to it, lest in so doing the reality be sacrificed to mere wishful thinking.

Even these German reports, while bringing into prominence every case of unrest and discontent, in places suggest a general impression which is different from that conveyed by a mere summation of the individual incidents recorded. Compare the following report recorded under the general heading "From the Industrial Undertakings":

Saxony

"As a general rule one can say that the older workers are tired and without much hope, whereas the younger ones are fanatically inclined and firmly convinced of Germany's superiority."[1]

Now it is clear from the foregoing chapters that the practical outcome of the social policy of National Socialist Germany is something very far removed from a workers' paradise. To do the leaders justice they have never claimed that the New Germany of the future, to which they bid the masses lift their eyes, could be built without sacrifice and hardship in the present. Long hours, hard work, frugality and privation—"let these be thy Gods", say the Nazis, "until better times arise and Germany can come into her rightful heritage among the nations". It is doubtless true that the fact, that in order to obtain this heritage smaller nations must be trampled underfoot and their independence and liberties suppressed, is viewed with mixed feelings by important sections of the population. But it is not plausible to

[1] *Germany. Monthly Reports of the Executive Committee of the S.D.P.* Vol. IV, 1940, No. 2, p. 44.

suppose that even the German workers (still less the rest of the German people) can regard the triumphant progress of Hitlerian diplomacy, or the successes of German arms now that it has come to war, in the same light in which they appear to the vanquished States, or to ourselves who are offering a stout, and it is devoutly to be hoped, a successful resistance to the Nazi pretensions to European and perhaps World domination by Germany. The German worker is not merely a worker, he is also a *German*, and he has not forgotten the last war and the Treaty of Versailles. While, therefore, not imputing to the German workers the chauvinism of their rulers, it seems reasonable to assume that it has not proved too difficult to persuade them that there are reasons of State policy (cf. "a strong Germany", "freedom from the servitude of Versailles" and similar slogans) why they should submit willingly to hardships at the moment—and this the more naturally as their only knowledge of European affairs is derived from their own Press and wireless. The average German has a tremendously strong "community sense", and he is very ready to respond when this is appealed to, even though he knows that it will involve much personal sacrifice.

Viewed objectively, the case against the social

policy of National Socialist Germany rests on sins of commission and on sins of omission. Under the former head come, for example, the suppression of the trade unions and of the right to strike; the authoritarian regulation of wages, hours and working conditions; the virtual conscription of labour in the early part of 1939 while peace was still continuing; and the enforced lengthening of hours of work to ten, twelve or more a day.

Taking the first of these major charges, the suppression of the trade unions and of the right to strike, the direct reaction upon the workers themselves of this loss of their former rights must be largely influenced by the immediate past history of the trade unions, and by the way in which the alternative machinery of control of industrial relations has functioned. There were three trade union organisations in Germany which did not pull very well together, and inside the one with much the largest membership—the "Free" or Socialist trade union—there was bitter dissension between the radical, communist wing and the more moderate section to which most of the trade union officials belonged. During the depression after 1930 the unions lost heavily in membership; except where they were backed by the State labour officials (*Schlichter*) or by a Mediation Board, they were powerless to resist the employers over wage reductions; and in general they had suffered enormously in prestige amongst the body of workers. Moreover during the later years of the Weimar Republic the State had become more and more the ultimate arbiter in wage matters, and finally by the Emergency Decrees of 1931 had completely over-ridden all existing collective agreements. On the other hand the new machinery of wage regulation, the Labour Trustees, secured a more widespread observance of the ruling wage determinations than had been possible under the former system of collective bargaining; employment and earnings increased, and in many directions conditions of life and work improved greatly in comparison with the slump of 1930–32. These were the material benefits, and as is understandable they bulked large in the eyes of the German workers; but they were achieved at a great price— the loss of the ultimate foundation for any free participation of labour in the economic system.[1]

It was not until 1938–39 that the potentialities of the new method of regulating industrial relations for worsening the conditions of labour, came to be widely felt. It is on this latter phase that much of the criticism has very naturally fastened. Beginning with the construction of the Western Wall in the summer of 1938

[1] See above, p. 51.

and continuing with the Decrees of March 1939 and the still more drastic provisions on the outbreak of the war, the control over civilian labour became finally as complete as that over the conscript in the armed forces. The facts here are not in dispute, but the gravamen of the charge rests to a large extent on the introduction of many of these controls during a period of peace. It may, however, reasonably be observed that from the Munich crisis onwards Germany felt herself to be on the brink of war. The fact that it was her own deliberate foreign policy which had brought about this state of things does not render this statement any the less true. The old Latin tag— *inter arma silent leges*—is above all true of social policy. It is scarcely an exaggeration to say that there is no social policy in war time other than that which is dictated by more or less immediate considerations of productivity and output. The German rulers drew the logical deductions from the situation and cancelled a large part of their social policy on the ground of the national emergency. The British and French, whose policy was opposed to that of Hitler (the rightness of this is not, of course, in question), did not draw the logical deductions from their policy, with the result that they entered the war in a lamentably unprepared condition. It was not in fact until

June and July 1940 that powers of control over
labour, so closely similar to those taken over
twelve months earlier by Germany that they seem
to have been copied from the latter, were finally
taken. When Dr Robson says that the employed
masses of German men and women "have entered
a state of peonage, the like of which has not
been seen in the countries of Western Europe for
centuries", he would seem to lay himself open
to the counter-charge that the same statement
could be applied to the British worker in July 1940.
Between the measures appropriate to a condition
of "near war" and those appropriate to a condition of actual war, there may be a difference in
point of degree, but hardly in point of kind.[1]

The remarks just made apply substantially to
the hardships resulting from the extension of
hours of work in all those industries which were
directly connected with the war effort. All ordinary restrictions, based on grounds of humanity,
the health and well-being of the workers, and
their desires, were swept aside on the ground of
the paramount necessity of securing maximum
output in the immediate moment, just as they

[1] The fact that the trade unions have great power in Britain,
and that those engaged in the administration of the British
Emergency Laws cannot go beyond what the unions will
tolerate, does constitute a real difference *in practice* between
German and British conditions.

were in this country in June and July 1940. In so far as subsequently there have been reductions in hours of work, they have been influenced, not by considerations of social policy, but solely by the limitations of human endurance to go on working excessive hours over long periods. In Great Britain long hours have been sweetened for the workers by very heavy overtime rates, but the National Socialists have had the harder task of enforcing overtime with relatively little extra pay. As has been shown in Chapter IV even their powers over labour broke down when they tried, and failed, to abolish overtime pay altogether. Nobody could pretend that excessive hours of work are popular with labour, but the available evidence goes to show that down to September 1939 the National Socialist régime had succeeded in persuading the German workers of the necessity, on national grounds, of working longer hours than they would have wished to do under normal conditions.

What has been said above is, of course, in no sense to be taken as an apologia for the National Socialists; but it is a plea for the importance of distinguishing between the social policy of normal times and the labour policy adopted by a government in war time or any period of national emergency.

At this point it becomes necessary to extend

the scope of the term social policy to include certain aspects of general policy which are of such wide application as to influence and affect almost every side of life.

In the view of the present writer one of the most serious of all the charges that can legitimately be levied against the social policy of Hitler's Germany is the existence of the Secret Police with their arbitrary powers of arrest and punishment, without recourse being possible to the normal processes of established law. This is the dark shadow which at all times since 1933 has hung over Germany. It directly concerns the worker because, in addition to the normal liability to dismissal, there is the further risk that any unguarded word or action in opposition to his employer may be construed as having political significance, and may lead to the intervention of the Secret Police. Fortunately for human happiness it is possible to get accustomed even to a perpetual dark shadow, and it may be doubted whether the average German worker is as acutely conscious of it in his daily life as the foreign observer is apt to imagine. Nevertheless, so long as the Secret Police and the concentration camps continue in being, the mere fact of their existence constitutes a shame and a reproach to the new German order.

Secondly, the spiritual enslavement of the German people—the imposed uniformity of thought and opinion—would seem to be so great a step backwards in civilisation that it must colour almost any assessment of a social policy, of which this spiritual enslavement forms an integral part— as it certainly does in the eyes of the Nazi leaders themselves.

A further charge of great weight, though of a rather different order, is the inhuman treatment of the Jews and of all those who have even a slight trace of Jewish blood in their veins. The whole "non-Aryan" population of Germany has been degraded to form a class of outcasts, to whom the normal social policy of Germany does not apply. Their standard of living has been deliberately depressed until, for the greater number, life in Germany has become an intolerable burden.

Not all those, however, who condemn Nazi Germany utterly on the first two counts in the foregoing indictment, remember that they are equally applicable to Soviet Russia.

Turning now to the sins of omission, Germany is charged, as has been noted in particular in the case of housing, with having sacrificed the standard of living of her people in order to pursue a policy of territorial aggrandisement. Here a distinction must be drawn between the period before and after September 1939. So long as Hitler's foreign policy was successful in bringing gains to Germany without involving the country in war, so long, for reasons stated earlier in this chapter, he carried his people with him even though they knew they had to pay a price for it. But he promised peace with bloodless victories, and yet in the end he led his people into war. Although unfortunately the Polish issue, which proved the *casus belli*, was of all possible causes the one most calculated to unite the entire German people behind Hitler, it still remains true that he failed to maintain peace, and this is likely to be held against him when the memory of his early conquests has become dim, and the hardships of a protracted war are pressing increasingly upon the population.

But if we consider only the period before 1939, then the National Socialists were surely in a strong position in relation to their own people. With all the forces of propaganda and publicity at their back, they could stress the much that they had undoubtedly achieved, while conveniently ignoring the more that they might have done. They could point above all to the conquest of unemployment, to the success of their population policy, to the extension of holidays with pay combined with the activities of *Kraft durch Freude*, to the improvement in the condition of the home workers, the care of the poor by Winter Relief, to developments in social insurance, and to the large housing programme. What had been left undone could always be attributed to the unfavourable situation in which Germany had found herself as a result of her defeat and the Peace Treaties.

Such contentions may stand the régime in good stead when it is presenting its balance sheet to the German people, but they do not alter the objective fact, which cannot be gainsaid, that rearmament, especially in 1938–39, was carried to such lengths that by far the greater part of the potential gains from full employment was sacrificed to the Moloch of preparation for war. Social policy, in the strict sense of the term, was the greatest sufferer, since it was perpetually subordinated to, and limited by, the over-riding claims of the military machine. Subject, however, to these vital limitations, it is but justice to recognise that the aims of social policy were kept continually in view and furthered as far as circumstances would permit. Nor is the record of the régime by any means devoid of achievement in this sphere.

Finally it should be emphasised that foreign policy has always been regarded in Germany since 1933 as in a peculiar sense the sole province of Hitler. Neither the people as a whole, nor the great majority of the important Party leaders, or

even some members of the Government, were
consulted when the crucial decisions were made.
On the other hand, millions of Germans were
drawn into the social policy of the Third Reich,
and could feel that they had a part to play in
building up a new and better Germany. How
far the inner ring of National Socialist leaders
were genuine and sincere in their pronouncements
in this respect must remain a matter of opinion;
but there can be no question at all that the enthusiasm and idealism of very large numbers of
people in Germany, above all the youth, were
captured by the "socialist" half of National
Socialist ideology. The inner ring of leaders may
have had their tongues in their cheeks when they
talked about *Gemeinnutz vor Eigennutz* (the interest
of the community before the interest of the individual), the dignity of manual labour, the new
social order with equality of opportunity without
the old class distinctions,[1] and with economic
security, and the like; but millions of Germans
have, in fact, been inspired by these ideas and have
devoted themselves—often with great self-sacrifice
—to the task of realising them, with that revo-
lutionary zeal, that faith that they can move

[1] The Nazis, however, are engaged in building up a new
system of class distinctions based on position and rank within
the National Socialist hierarchy.

mountains, which has been one of the outstanding features of National Socialist Germany.
And they have accomplished much that was
socially valuable and abundantly worth doing.

Modern Germany is a highly complex phenomenon,[1] with much that is good and bad in it,
and nothing is achieved except distortion and
absence of reality by any attempt to reduce it to
a simple picture of a vast population deluded and
oppressed by a small number of brutal gangsters.
The gangsters are there, but so also are those who
are moved by sincere ideals of social service
when they support the Nazi cause—a cause which
is abhorrent to most of us in this country (quite
apart from the war) because it repudiates and
seeks to destroy many of the values in life which
we cherish and hold most dear.

[1] How complex a phenomenon present-day Germany is, if
only from the political and psychological point of view, appears
from a recent and very instructive book by Mr Sebastian
Haffner, *Germany: Jekyll and Hyde*.

INDEX